Walter Southgate

That's the way it was

A working class autobiography 1890-1950

Walter Southgate

Edited with an afterword 1950-1981
by Terry Philpot

New Clarion Press
1982
in association with
History Workshop
Centre for London History

Published in 1982 by
New Clarion Press
11 Silkham Road Oxted Surrey RH8 0NP

ISBN 0 9507961 0 7

Printed in Great Britain by Pensord Press Ltd
Old Tram Road, Pontllanfraith
Blackwood, Gwent

To Grace

Editor's note

This book is an edited version of a much larger manuscript. The present volume has been assembled by excising repetitious passages and some incidents and remarks that could not find space given the requirements of length. At the same time the editor has added a few footnotes to assist readers, made minor corrections of detail and fact and carried out some reordering of the text to retain the flow and chronology of the book. None of this, he hopes, has been done at the expense of the book as a whole, and every attempt has been made to retain the flavour, the character, the wit, and the vigour of Walter Southgate's writing and of the life, times and activities which he describes. If this is apparent to the reader, then the editor will consider that his task has been satisfactorily dispatched.

The author and editor would like .to thank Stan Newens and Denis Hutchings for their help and encouragement.

Terry Philpot
January 1982

Foreword
Stan Newens MP

East London is today something of a legend — a place of strong political traditions, mythical working class consciousness and fascinating kinship patterns. For more than a century it has been a draw to sympathetic social investigators and reformers. However, its own natives, bred and born, though voluble in speech, have been less inclined to record their experiences in print. Now that the communities of which they were members in the heroic age are sadly passing away, some of the survivors are at last telling their own stories from the inside, as it were.

Walter Southgate is at the same time both a typical and a rare East End specimen. Born at Cambridge Heath more than a generation before the outbreak of the First World War of local working class stock, he knew life as it existed for the teeming thousands of East Enders in the closing decade of Victoria's reign and the Edwardian period.

Unlike many of them, however, Walter was a hoarder of relics and remains. He preserved a priceless scrapbook begun by his grandmother in the 1840s, which many of his contemporaries would have consigned to the dustbin. He kept pamphlets purchased from long-forgotten bookstalls for a few pence. He meticulously collected personal papers, political ephemera, prized possessions and various other curiosities over the years.

As a result he was able to make an invaluable contribution to the basic stock of the National Museum of Labour History which he helped a dedicated group of enthusiasts to establish in East London in 1975 and of which he was treasurer until 1978.

Walter was particularly fitted for this role as one of the pioneers of the early twentieth century Labour movement. No doubt influenced by his father's radicalism from which he made an early transition to socialism, he first joined the Social Democratic Federation led by Henry Mayer Hyndman, a top-hatted Marxist who had known the author of *Das Kapital* in person. Later as a founder member of the Hackney branch of the National Union of Clerks and a delegate to the Hackney Trades Council, Walter found himself deeply involved in the work of the Labour Representation Committee and the young Labour Party after its birth in 1906, and today he is one of its oldest living members.

In the days before the First World War it was by no means common for a working class youth in London, which was then politically much less advanced than the industrial areas of the North, to commit himself to the socialist cause. Few people questioned the order of things as they found them and those who did were regarded by their fellows with the same sense of outrage and distaste as those born in to more affluent circumstances.

On working class conditions in East London at the turn of the century, and on its culture and the way of life of its people, Walter's testimony is invaluable. His description of housing conditions and sanitary facilities, the role of the public house, the pawnshop, of children's street games, religion, and the schools is specific to the community in which he lived. He tells his story with the cockney wit which has never left him.

History used to be the study of the lives and activities of the great and the wealthy, but today it is increasingly realised that ordinary people have their history, which is in many ways more basic and fundamental. The enormous transformation of life in this country which has taken place in the twentieth century can only be understood by the study of their lives.

It is not enough, however, to do this impersonally as if people can be regarded as mere conglomerations of social actions — masses to be manipulated by leaders whether proletarian or of the privileged classes. It is now clear that individual cultural patterns and the multifarious features of communities are of great significance in the way that historical change occurs.

London's role in the development of modern Britain has been badly misunderstood by many historians who have underestimated the importance of regional variations. We need to know more of life at the grassroots if the record is to be corrected. Walter Southgate, in this absorbing and entertaining account of the East End he knew and of his life as an activist in the Labour and trades union movement, has encapsulated in print a grassroots memory that would otherwise not survive. Rough hewn and unpolished though in some respects it may be, its authenticity and sincerity, which truly reflect the personal qualities and integrity of the author and a lifetime of constructive activity, give this book a value which will increase with the passage of the years.

Chapter 1

I was born on 8 May 1890 at 49, North Street*, Cambridge Heath, a street next to the Regent's Canal. Across the canal from our cottage was Bethnal Green with its turnpike which in days past had opened the way to Whitechapel and Shoreditch. Our house was a slum, one of a long row of brick boxes with holes in them for two doors and four windows, of a kind which in those days smothered the East End. There were four rooms and a small back yard. We called it "home".

The front door abutted the pavement, and the front window was draped with curtains to stop peeping Toms looking into what we called the front parlour, which was more often than not used as a bedroom. Through the window one might discern a big round table displaying a photo album with brass clasps or a large Bible alongside a potted aspidistra.

The Bible was purely for show, a hallmark of respectability. Few adults in the East End attended church except for the three ceremonies of their lives — baptism, marriage and burial. Of the first and the last they were not conscious at the time, and of the second most male participants were half drunk at the time it took place.

My father was William Southgate and my mother had been Elizabeth Bickley before their marriage. I came into the world at a period when my father was out of work for a short time. My mother was going out charing up to a fortnight before I arrived, to bring food into the home. Then there was no help like social security benefits or maternity care. East Enders relied on themselves and help from their neighbours.

For a day's charing my mother was paid three shillings (15p) with one meal provided. The doctor was late in arriving, mother told me later, so little Tiny Henshaw acted as an unofficial midwife, one of a number of women who did so in the East End in those days (just as my mother helped in the same way on many occasions for neighbours). Later on my mother told me I was born with a caul, and she asserted that this was a lucky omen as I would never drown because of this. But nevertheless I learnt to swim to make certain that she was right.

Tiny Henshaw was also my godmother, although I did not know this until I was 14. Being a godparent was a matter of form among the working class. Tiny had her own domestic troubles throughout her life without the added burden of looking after my religious and spiritual

*now Northiam Street

upbringing or the giving of presents as dictated by custom in a more privileged society. When I was 14, I also learnt that my second forename was Charles (which mother had completely forgotten). It was only when I found my birth certificate tucked away in one of mother's favourite wedding vases on the parlour mantlepiece, where she also kept her pawn tickets and other personal knick-knacks, that I made my discovery. The casualness of it all seemed an afront to my ego.

At christening ceremonies fathers and other males were rarely present. That would be beneath their dignity. Fathers did not push perambulators with babies through the streets, for it, too, would be considered beneath their dignity, a comedown in the realm of cockney family life. Tiny was heard to remark before admiring females, when I was unwrapped from my swaddling clothes (borrowed for the occasion from friendly neighbours): "E's the dead spit of 'is farver", which was interpreted as a compliment to my Dad. "He'd better be", remarked my father, "or there'll be ructions if he ain't".

My mother said that in my ways I grew up to be like my Grandfather Southgate in all sorts of ways. I had to take her word for it (especially as she said nice things about him) for he had died broken in health and unable to work four years before I was born.

My father was 21 and mother was 20 when they married at St John's Church, Bethnal Green on 15 June, 1874. That it had been a love match I know from the day when my mother was turning out the contents of that cherished vase of hers. She tipped the articles on to the table amongst which were some out of date pawn tickets and a few trinkets and wax flowers retrieved from the bridal wedding cake of long ago. Handling her faded relics rather fondly she remarked: "Do you know son, I married yer father for love. I 'ad several blokes arter me becorse I was a pretty girl then, although I say it as shouldn't. If I 'ad married for money I could 'ave 'ad Mr. F . . . ." (mentioning the name of a large boot manufacturer who I knew had a large factory at Tottenham and had started in business in a very small way in the East End of London). "Then I would not have been here", I remarked. "Perhaps yes, and perhaps no, son," she replied. "More likely yer would have 'ad a bigger konk [nose] an' more toffee apples than yer get now. Instead yer 'ave to put up wiv patches on yer backside 'elping yer ol' mum to run errands."

My parents had seven children, three of them dying when young. In 1814 my paternal great-grandfather, John Southgate became a freeman of the City of Norwich. In the parchment deed he is described as a silk weaver. My Grandfather George in time was also a freeman. He, in turn, in 1853, was described as a cord spinner. He afterwards became a cordwainer or shoemaker and migrated to London about the 1860s because work was scarce in his native town. He settled around the Haggerston area, the centre of the boot and shoe industry. Visible evidence of his work lay about our cottage when I was a boy, in the shape of a number of wooden lasts which he fashioned out of wood blocks to the shape of individuals' feet — surgical cases mostly. These lasts gradually disappeared to feed the kitchen fire. I still possess his boxwood sliding rule measure from which they were made. Grandfather George was also a man of radical opinions. My maternal grandfather, George Bickley, was also a shoemaker and was born about the 1830s in a small thatched cottage on Springhill, Upper Clapton, now part of the local authority park. He died when I was a schoolboy, but I can just remember him as a small frail old man who died as poor as he was born. His wife, my maternal grandmother, was built of sterner stuff. She was born at Epping Green. Her mother, a Mrs Candler, died when Granny was about 11 years old, leaving six younger children whom Granny helped to bring up. When and how she came to live in Bethnal Green I never knew. The metropolis was a magnet when country workers were striken by poverty in the days of agricultural depression.

Granny Bickley had grit and courage for in between having children of her own to bring up, she ran a small babies' footware business in the front room of her house near the Columbia Market, Bethnal Green.

My grandmother's business continued with varying fortune until her husband's death when she went to live with her son, Walter, at Walthamstow. I remember her as an independent old lady working at her boot machine without the aid of glasses until she was well past 80, travelling to and from Liverpool Street Station with her home work. She lived to be 91.

She had vivid memories of the Crimean War when the cost of living was high against the wages paid and there was great distress among the poor. She told of the appalling scandals surrounding war contracts and the callous treatment of our soldiers and the brave efforts of Florence Nightingale on behalf of our wounded soldiers. She had witnessed the passing of the stage coach and the advent of radio. Asked what she thought was the greatest invention of her time, she said the telephone. "Not the wireless from Savoy Hill?" I asked and she said: "No". Manipulating the "cat's whisker" could hardly be called a "wireless" because it was all wires. The headphones were nothing but telephones.

Grandfather Southgate had a brother John, who emigrated to New Zealand about the same time he himself had come to London. My father said he went down to Tilbury to see his uncle and his cousins, Horace and Margaret, depart in an emigrant sailing ship. Letter writing between working class families then were practically non-existent, so between uncle and nephew one letter passed each way in 20 years. Apparently my father had thoughts of emigrating in the 1880s and wrote to his uncle. The latter's reply, in the handwriting of a professional character and hardly that of an aged relative, intimated to my father that his uncle had started as a tallow maker but was now a gardener. The sailing had taken six months to get across; the native Maoris had just finished their little war, people ate meat at every meal as there was plenty of it, Margaret had married a Mr Redshaw and had two children. He hadn't made a fortune but if father thought of coming out to New Zealand there was plenty of work. My father must have changed his mind about emigrating, which to me was a pity, as I feel sure if this had happened he would have gradually given up the lure of the East End public house life for something more engrossing and advantageous both for himself and his family, free from the sordidness of living it out in an East End slum.

Instead father opted to sign a three-year contract with a quill pen firm in Aberdeen of all places. He went up by boat, took mother with him for a time but she pined for home and relations, hated the granite look of the place and its weather. A cockney in Aberdeen was asking too much.

My New Zealand uncle left behind his son George, whom I visited as a youth once, my purpose being to find out more about my Norwich and New Zealand relations. My father was not in the least interested in them — and *vice versa.* This fellow George turned out to be a very talkative fellow, full of love and understanding for his native Norwich canaries and nothing else. He bred the birds in cages ranged around two top bedrooms in his Camden Town house. He earned a fair competence from the sale of his songsters. So obviously was he bound up with his canaries that what with his ceaseless chatter about feeding, breeding, training and showing off all their good points for the show bench, mingled with the twittering and singing of his birds, I came away as wise as I went about my relations. Father's comment was that I had got the bird.

Uncle Walter Bickley was a foreman cardboard box maker, my only uncle who was a total abstainer. He led a steady life with his wife and family. After his wife died things seemed to go to pieces. In the name of economy his firm sacked him when he was about 50 and like all of his age and class, in spite of his total abstaining from strong liquor, he became unemployable. He scratched along for some time and eventually married a widow with a shop and so saved his economic situation.

Uncle Bill Yorston was married to mother's sister Aunt Alice. He was an engineer but he forsook the craft and took up the making of boiled sweets. These he made in a backroom and scullery of a dingy little shop in a dingier little street of Hoxton. To supplement this activity, he kept a sweet stall in the nearby Nile Street market. He also made mineral waters in his back yard. This "Monster Pop", as it was called, was sold for a penny a large bottle, which had a glass marble in its twisted throat, which was forced down by pressure to release the liquid fizz. Really the concoction was nothing but sweetened water, a touch of coloured essence with a dosage of "gas" from the bottling machine to give it the fizz and pop. Hoxton kids loved it. Four of them would share a bottle at a farthing a swig.

The basis of most of Uncle Bill's sweets was glucose. Bags of this powder were stacked in his scullery. Long before the medical profession discovered them, Uncle Bill was supplying Hoxton children of all ages with heavy doses of vitamins at four ounces a penny. Uncle Bill also made jelly babies — in copper pans, of course — and sold them for four ozs a penny. They were made up from a concoction of gelatine, colouring powder and a few drops of essence flavouring. When in a plastic state the jelly went through a moulding machine followed by a dusting powder to prevent the various coloured "infants" amalgamating into one lump of indefinable colour. There were black babies, yellow babies, blue babies, red babies and colourless babies leading to arguments among children as to how many reds and black babies they got for their farthing before devouring them. Personally, I liked the black ones which were flavoured with liquorice, but the powder of that name sold at the chemist's, of which mother insisted that we kids should take a weekly dose, made me vomit at the very smell of it.

Uncle Bill also made crumpets. These were large, flat discs for a farthing each. It was really fried black treacle. Tamorine was a sticky substance dug out of a 14lb jar and spread on paper for a halfpenny. It had a sharp, sweet flavour. Stickjaw was a toffee, studded with slivers of coconut, and at the universal price of four ounces for a penny it was very popular with school boys. It lived up to its name. A boy caught with a lump in his mouth often found it stuck to his teeth and was unable to swallow it quickly. Locust beans (carob tree) and tiger nuts are also no longer to be found in sweet shops.

One other money-making gimmick of Uncle Bill's was the lucky sawdust dip. For a farthing you were allowed to dip into a wooden tub filled with sawdust and extract one small stick of rock, covered in tissue paper, from the many buried within it. If the rock had a coloured stripe running through it you were entitled to a pennyworth of sweets from anywhere in the shop, and a penny to a Hoxton child was a week's pocket money. Uncle Bill kept count of the number of plain and coloured rocks that went in and out of his tub, and the odds were about 50 to one, a more certain price than Uncle Bill ever got from putting his shirt on the favourite in the 2.30 at Newmarket.

My mother's sister Alice was a sad case of dipsomania, a not uncommon complaint when spirits were so cheap. She never entered a public house, being a secret drinker. Many were the strategems employed to get children to obtain for her the half quart of gin (then costing about 2½d) from the local public houses (as in those days children were allowed to do). I was one of the children whom she pressed into service. The spirit was commonly known as ''mother's ruin'' and in her case it was literally true as she died eventually of alcoholic poisoning.

I had another Uncle Bill, a silversmith and glass beveller by trade who was married to another of my mother's sisters. He was an unobtrusive man, not a great talker, which suited father. Both of them bosom pals on regular Sunday morning ''traveller'' jaunts on their round of public houses outside the three mile limit*. At such public houses around the Hackney Marshes they would produce an old frayed tram or train ticket to prove to the potman through the half-opened door that they were *bona fide* ''travellers'' within the meaning of the law.

Then there was Uncle Fred Fricker, married to another of mother's sisters. He was a coachman to a commercial traveller for wholesale drapers. Uncle Fred looked quite smart sitting on his dicky box seat with his white cravat and highly polished top hat, with a cockade. The coach was a four-wheeler.

Inside the coach were dozens of cardboard boxes containing samples of lingerie, and so on. Accompanying them was the frock-coated, high-hatted traveller cooped up amongst his boxes just like a sardine in a tin box and feeling like one I expect. Uncle Fred must have been a tough character as he was out in all weathers. He kept his horse and coach in tip top condition.

As to my other antecedents there was my paternal great-grandfather James Yaxley who was a farm bailiff or steward and came from a family of boat builders around Barton Broad, Norfolk. Apparently he was a careful and saving man for he bought a house-cum-village shop, nine acres of land, together with six cottages in the village of Smallburgh, Norfolk. He married twice and had 10 daughters. The eldest of three daughters by his first wife was my grandmother, Mary Ann Yaxley. Her father before his death in about 1880, made a well-intentioned will leaving something for all his progeny. But as he left his second wife a life interest in the village property and made no provision as to its proper maintenance for the ultimate benefit of his offspring, the property became neglected and fell into disrepair.

His second wife lived to be 90 years old. Tenants of the six cottages had paid no rent for several years because of their condition. Finally the council stepped in, took one look and the cottages were demolished.

---

*In those days the licensing laws forbade Sunday drinking in public houses except for *bona fide* travellers who were three miles from home. Thus those travelling away from home for a drink would have to produce a tram or bus ticket for the barman.

When I went to view my "ancestral home" in 1920 the house and shop had been repaired and sold but all I could see of the cottages was a pile of old bricks and rubble. Considering the area that must have been covered they must have been very primitive with stone age amenities. I suppose the old lady saw no architectural beauty, romance or rent to justify their survival and had no money of her own to endow the numerous descendents of her long-departed husband.

My grandmother, born in this Smallburgh cottage-cum-shop, died six years before I was born. My mother said she was a charming old dear. I like to think so too, judging from the cuttings and illustrations my grandmother pasted into a big scrapbook in the 1840s.

The final distribution of James Yaxley's estate took place 26 years after his second wife's death. When he died he had left a will leaving all his property to his second wife on trust, and stipulating that on her death property was to be sold and divided between all descendents of his two marriages. The old lady lived to a ripe old age and the result was that great-grandfather Yaxley's descendants being numerous and his estate being modest, those of his family still living came into exactly 15s 9d each.

Chapter 2

''Sir, if you wish to have a just notion of the magnitude of this City, you must not be satisfied with seeing its great streets and squares, but must survey the innumerable little lanes and courts''

Dr Johnson's observation was recorded by James Boswell but whole districts have been embraced into London since the doctor's days. Where, in his time, there were acres of grass, cornfields and market gardens, by the time I went to school in the 1890s there were acres upon acres of brick boxes. There had now arisen a vast forest of chimney pots, belching forth soot and smoke to hide the glorious sun; streets teemed with people, carts, carriages, horses, dung and flies so that the demand in summer for fly papers had become a regular trade for street hawkers and small shopkeepers. It was now an area where public houses stood on almost every street corner. Parishes like those of Hackney and Islington and numerous others were pleasant little villages at the time Dr Johnson made his commentary and remained so until about 1820, and, in some cases, even later.

The cottages in North Street, Bethnal Green, where I was born, were typical of many thousands of others throughout the East End. Father said that our cottages were built about 1830-40 for brickmakers employed around the district known as Bonner's Fields, stretching as far as Old Ford and Hackney Wick and named after Bishop Bonner who lived in the reign of Henry VIII. In that street there were about 100 cottages similar in pattern and built in a continuous row each with a 12 feet frontage to the street and with a front door opening immediately onto the pavement. When I was a boy each cottage had wooden shutters to the one and only window on the ground floor and they were religiously shut and bolted every night. They ensured privacy and excluded air from the room, which in most cases was used as a bedroom at night. During the daytime it became the front parlour.

Each cottage had four rooms, two up and two down, each set respectively measuring 12 feet by 10 feet and 12 feet by 8 feet. There was also an outside wooden outhouse covering a brick copper, used for boiling the family linen, Christmas puddings, and the like. In our own family, father also used it for ''dutching'' his quill feathers in hot silver sand prior to their being cut for pens.

The backyards were all alike (you could hardly call them gardens, although many were the efforts some cottagers made to bring anaemic looking plants into flower in a sunless zone). The yard measured 12 feet by 16 feet and contained a back-to-back WC in which it was possible to hold a conversation with the occupant next door. The water tap was also in this back yard open to the weather and subject to freeze-ups. At the rear of the yard was a very high brick wall over which looked elm trees, planted by the owners of the "better class" on the other side. Trees and wall also served to hide from view those awful people of North Street and their brick boxes. Tenants on the other side of North Street fared no better. They had similar-sized yards and instead of a high wall they had high stacks of timber and the company of canal rats.

On occasions when our parents' backs were turned we boys would often climb those elm trees to top their branches without so much as asking leave of the owners. Sometimes we threw over this wall a few tin cans always explaining that it was to scare the tom cats from serenading one another and disturbing our sleep. Our dead cats and dogs, who had been our pets, were decently buried in our own backyard with an appropriate cross to mark the spot; this is, until a new tenant took possession and upset this memorial.

In the back yard father had his "grotto", a beloved Victorian garden ornament wedged between the brick WC and the coal box. He had built it of old bricks, chunks of clinker refuse, scallop shells and broken glass and chinaware ornaments. It was not a good example of garden architecture but it was one up on old Mr Sayers down the road, who quite blatantly inserted in his "grotto" old chamber pots in which he grew creeping jenny.

Every year father planted a few geraniums and blue lobelia plants but with the soot, lack of sun and cinder ash in the soil they lingered to a premature death. Nevertheless he persisted and encouraged mother to plant her favourite pot of musk (which had scent in those days) and creeping jenny. If a tuft of grass appeared in the crevices of stones and clinker she would tend it as if it was a lily so divorced totally was she from the country scene. It reminded her, she said, "of the country". Apart from the four horse brake outing to High Beech in Epping Forest or Theydon Bois, run by the local publican for his customers once a year, this was about as much of the country as my mother saw.

Each Sunday morning every housewife in the street cleaned her front doorstep, and the paving stone on the public pavement was hearthstoned. If there was a brass knocker on the door, this too was polished. Usually these tasks fell upon the daughters of the household. The women took a great interest in their front room curtains.

No one could boast of a letter box so that the "rat a tat tat" of the postman was indeed an event everybody knew about. There would be enquiries as to whether it was good or bad news. Letter boxes were a sign of affluence and status in those days. Boys of the street would have had no end of fun playing with them as we certainly did with door knockers, in our game of ''knocking down, Ginger'' with a few boys in a line running through the street banging on the door knockers.

The rents of those cottages were around five shillings per week. In relation to the worker's wage packet the rent was dear. Such property was owned principally by petty successful tradesmen who did little in the way of repairs. The tenants who had some regard for fresh whitewash and wallpaper would do this on their own account, putting paper on paper but never getting rid of the ''mahogany backs'' (bugs).

Father was always ready to air his views about the rent racket having read his Henry George and other social reformers of his time. When father said he had ''paid for the cottage 10 times over'' this was clearly an understatement. ''When these cottages were built about 1840'', he would say ''they were erected in a continuous row with standardised doors, frames, fittings, etc. and could not have cost more than £30 to £40 a piece. Over all the years'', he continued ''I have lived here the repairs have been negligible. The whole place is just brick walls and wooden frames: the cottages are holding each other up, one big bang and they will all fall down''.

But this is as far as father ever got with his radical arguments at the ''four ale bar'' or with me as the only listener at home. Many of his public house listeners were ignorant of politics and voteless into the bargain, so father's claim about ''legalised robbery'' fell mainly on deaf ears. His advocacy that all land should belong to the nation (nationalisation) as a basic solution to our housing problem was considered a crackpot socialist idea. With successive Labour governments it has remained a ''hot potato''.

One of my earliest recollections was of an arson case when I must have been between the age of four and five years old. My mother, relating the story in later life, said that I worried the life out of her because I wanted to go to school with my sister, Florence, aged six. I cried and stamped my feet when I was told that I was not of legal age of five. Apparently I got so much on my mother's nerves that she decided to see the headmistress of the infants department of Mowlem Street Elementary School at Cambridge Heath. ''Very well'' said the headmistress ''We have discretionary rules that under fives can be admitted on odd days to accustom infants to school surroundings and discipline.'' ''Breaking the colt in'', said father, ''but I'll bet it will cure him after a few days''. How right he was! Playing truant from school was a problem in the East End of those days so the under-fives rule was an attempt to cushion the problem. Moreover, it was always drummed into us by our parents that habitual truants were given over to special places called reformatory schools where the discipline was harsh and strict and you were taken away from your parents. I remember that there was one such reformatory in nearby Clapton and it looked formidable to me, more like a barracks surrounded by tall iron railings and boys marching about in squads and drilling like soldiers all the time.

Mother dressed me up in my best knicker-bocker suit as it would not do for a first occasion to send me in my usual pair of father's cut-down trousers with a patch on the backside. My sister held my hand and kept repeatedly telling me to behave myself as we walked to school over the canal bridge and through several streets before we came to Mowlem Street School. This was an awesome building, one of the first to be erected by the London School Board about the 1870s with all three departments — infants, boys and girls. "The boy was quite happy and cheerful", mother said, "as he went along to school, quite a little lamb", and added afterwards: "But he came back a roaring brat". What had happened?

I was introduced to the lady teacher who placed me at the back of the class alongside my sister, Florence. The teacher gave me some coloured pencils and a sheet of paper to play with. How well I remember those pencils. I must have got tired playing with them and like all boys began searching my pockets for the odd marble and any kind of old rubbish little boys cherish. Instead, I found a lucifer match. It was about three inches long, fairly thick and, when struck on any rough surface, would burst into flames and emit a nasty, sulphurous odour.

The coloured pencils having lost interest for me, the easiest thing was to play with the newly discovered match stick, which I found had a real live head to it. I rubbed it up and down on the iron work of the school desk just as I had seen my father do when he lit up for his pipe. Suddenly there was a flash, the match was alight, stinking horribly. My sister screamed out: "Oh!". The class shouted: "Look", and the next thing I knew I was pounced upon by the teacher, and given a sharp rap over the knuckles with the coloured pencils. She sent me home immediately with my sister and a note to mother that, under no circumstances, could the school admit me until I was five.

When I was five, I was admitted — my crime forgotten — and I stayed at the same school until I was 14. I won a gold medal for not being late or absent once in seven years, as well as winning many book prizes and award cards for studies and I continued with evening classes until I was 17 years of age.

The one remarkable fact about my North Street residence, as with so many hundreds of East End street communities, was the community spirit that existed. I experienced and witnessed numerous examples of the cockney's indomitable spirit in adversity. This was mainly because family life was closely knit, attached to mother, the linchpin of the family wheel. Nothing was done without mother being consulted. Even her grown up sons bowed to her long after they were married. Her daughters when married would never live too far from her, so that mother was always on hand to help and advise; grandchildren worshipped her, paying regular homage and visits to Granny. The family would move heaven and earth rather than she should finish her last days in the workhouse as a pauper, too often unfortunately the fate of many when times were especially bad.

Another feature of that community spirit was that neighbours settled their disputes and differences without resort to the law. They had great respect for the police but shut up like clams whenever the law began to pry.

Of course, trouble arose in such crowded streets and alleyways, overrun with children getting into all sorts of mischief where the street was their only playground. A great deal of bad language would fly around, aspersions made about one's character and doubtful family relations called into question. It might come to blows, a black eye or hair torn out but never were knives or other dangerous weapons used. After some time had elapsed there would be a reconciliation, several glasses of beer — sometimes called pig's ear — or a glass of ''mother's ruin'' drunk to close the episode.

In that kind of close community in which we lived there could not be enmity for long for mutual aid was the keystone of existence when difficult times came along and had to be faced. In the presence of strangers and the police the cockney knew nothing, saw nothing and heard nothing and out of that, nothing can be made. One curious thing I noticed as a child was that although our parents and others used a great deal of swear words, even in front of their own children, yet it was a strict rule that children must not use such language on pain of dire punishment.

Chapter 3

As families were packed closely together in their little brick boxes, it was possible to know a great many of each of their skeletons. There were a few families, however, who tried to keep themselves in isolation from the rest. They preferred to suffer the pangs of hunger and distress within their own four walls. Poverty to them was something to be ashamed of; it should be hidden away from the vulgar gaze of neighbours. Calamity would sometimes overtake them when the skeletons, which they had been hiding, would be taken out for neighbours to see. The bailiffs or broker's men would enter and possess a few articles of furniture to cover the arrears of rent. Sometimes there would be a ''moonlight flit'' in a covered van to avoid this happening. In those days there was no difficulty in finding vacant rooms or premises. Agents' boards announcing ''To Let'' could be seen in almost every street.

I remember the broker's men in our own front parlour, considered by every respectable working class family as the holy of holies. My parents never looked upon poverty as a crime or as something to be ashamed of, neither did they adopt all sorts of subterfuge to make others think they were different to what they really were, poor and the victims of a bad economic system. They never moaned about it and just took life as it came, a philosophy not to everyone's taste. The presence of those bailiffs in our front parlour was, in my youthful eyes, however, a visit of men from the dark regions. They sat there in our parlour smoking their clay pipes and drinking beer from a tin can, which was replenished from time to time by each taking it in turns to visit the local public house. My mother would be busy going around to various neighbours, almost as poor as ourselves, for temporary small loans to save the bits and pieces of furniture that had been earmarked by the broker's men for removal by sundown.

It was Mrs Jacobs, who lived in North Street, who came to the rescue as she had done on other occasions. She had no money readily available but such was her natural disposition to help she had no hesitation in taking off her gold wedding ring, saying to mother: ''E're yer are, Liz, pawn it, and get it out, Sat'day''. Meanwhile she replaced the gold ring with a brass one, a most important thing to do this so that the prudish amongst her kind should not notice its absence and say: ''Fancy that brazen bitch walking about wiv'out 'er wedding ring on''.

Mrs Jacobs worked with extraordinary energy at her boot-sewing machine at home for a period. With the proceeds of her labour she would go on a shopping expedition to replenish her own and her children's wardrobe, finally winding up with a gin-drinking orgy. Her weakness for the gin bottle was shared by many women of her generation. Gin was cheap in those days and there was also a prevailing notion amongst them that it had contraceptive powers. Her first born son was a dwarf of three feet although all the rest of her children were quite normal physically. Her gin-drinking orgy reached a climax when she sought refuge in our cottage until she sobered up before facing her infuriated husband. While this episode was being enacted it was pathetic to watch ''little Tich'', as we called her dwarf son, acting as a sort of spy, going backwards and forwards between the two homes to discover whether it was safe to smuggle his now semi-sober mother into her house and bed before the irate husband returned from searching for her in the public houses. Sometimes the ruse failed for on the morrow it became apparent to all living in that street that the erring wife now possessed an eye of different hue. Such a painful spectacle never made the slightest difference to Mrs Jacobs, for she — and little Tich — would do the same all over again.

In spite of her weakness for the gin bottle, Mrs Jacobs had many sterling qualities: she never neglected her children, clothed them out of her own earnings, lending her gold wedding ring to pay my parents' rent which to me signified she was a woman of character and generosity.

Then there was Mrs Kellaway. One day her husband walked out of his cottage, never to return. Mrs Kellaway avoided any enquiries about him. All she would say was ''He gave no reasons'', and no one in that street knew of domestic quarrelling to account for this strange episode. She was left to face the hard economic struggle with four young children, a formidable task. Faced with the problem of the workhouse, her children taken from her, the home broken up, and the police were advised by the Poor Law Guardians to trace her husband.

With Mrs Kellaway's courage and determination she turned her front room into a little grindery shop, erected a few shelves and a counter and started to sell grindery goods, tobacco and anything else that promised business. Such an effort commanded neighbours' respect and custom. She never made a fortune; it must have been a struggle at times but she managed to live and keep her children until they were old enough to go out to work and help to keep themselves. Their father was a complete wash out and was never traced.

The streets of the East End were also the playgrounds of the children in the days of the horse and cart and hawker's barrows peddling their wares. Half a dozen kids trying to play games in their back yards would have driven any mother to distraction (''up the pole'' would be the exact expression) so mothers turned us children into the street to play when, of course, we developed all sorts of games which have now died out.

No games were allowed on Sundays but our games were linked with the seasons. We had no apparatus except what we improvised for ourselves — coats down in the road for goal posts; the lamp post for a cricket stump; a rough piece of wood shaped for a cricket bat; ''tibby cats'' fashioned from firewood; balls of pressed paper and string and glass marbles (called ''glarnies'', four a penny). There were caps down for ''egg if I move''; spinning tops; iron hoops for boys and wooden ones for girls; cherry stones for ''bobs''; ''conkers'' on string (proud was the boy who had a ''twentier'' from his ''kills''); five stones and hop scotch chalked on the pavement for girls. Occasionally, the games would be interrupted by a cart and horse driving through the street or the policeman would appear who frowned upon cricket and football as dangerous to neighbours' window panes.

On the pavement outside our cottage was the lamp post and each evening and morning the lamp lighter would come round and switch on and off the gas light with the aid of a long pole. This lamp post being outside our cottage my parents had free lighting for their bedroom, although during the day time it proved to be a nuisance to my mother who was always complaining about the street children using the lamp post for a cricket stump or the girls would sling a rope over its top arm to the peril of passersby and her window panes. In return for some free lighting throughout the years, we got a few cracked panes of glass and mother constantly said: ''You ought to do something about it''. But father never did and the lamp post stayed until the German bombs destroyed it in 1940.

When steam rollers were used to repair the roads, children from the safety of the pavement were fascinated with the effortless way the steam-roller ground all the small granite pieces to a flat surface that made a metalled road surface in those days. Children also took rides on the back of the horse-drawn water cart sprinkler, a necessity in those days of dusty roads, strewn with horse droppings. Should, however, the driver of this sprinkler cart catch a child taking a free ride, then beware of a sudden shower.

One of my boyish ambitions was to play with a horse-drawn fire engine with its array of pipes and shiny brass fittings. In my imagination I turned on the hose pipe. As children we ingratiated ourselves with the night watchman in the evening who allowed us to bake potatoes on his brazier fire. Simple pleasures for children, perhaps, but near enough to the redskin stories from the pages of Fenimore Cooper.

Our ambitions and dreams as children would be conditioned to a great measure by the social status of our parents. Therefore, I aspired to become an engineer or an engine driver at which my father had doubts. When I quoted to him that I had read ''that there is a field marshal's baton in every soldier's knapsack'' he replied that I should be lucky if I became an onion peeler in a pickle factory. My father had no illusions.

As I got a little older my passion for driving horse-drawn fire engines became dimmer and was finally extinguished with the advent of the motor powered engine. I had no love for motors or technical things, unlike my brother who loved mechanical gadgets. My dream was of holding the reins attached to a dashing pair of greys, racing through the streets with the firebell clanging, pulling up in the grand manner all lather and sweat outside the scene of the conflagration, climbing ladders at amazing speed, rushing through flame and smoke to rescue the fair damsel in the nick of time. All romantic stuff. I never thought then, in actual fact, that the damsel might turn out to be a 16 stone coster-monger's wife with six flannel petticoats. Nevertheless, I would receive the cheers of the crowd and a gold medal for my heroic behaviour—I hoped.

No doubt the romantic notions I got came from hearing the recital of the popular lines of the "Fireman's Wedding" at our local Band of Hope. At the age of 10, I had signed the pledge of total abstinence from alcoholic liquor and was made a captain and given a blue sash to signify my office to take charge of other youthful abstainers from alcohol.

It was at these weekly gatherings of total abstainers, who paid a halfpenny a week for under 12s, that we had songs and recitations coached by a dramatic youth who had come all the way from Oxford University in need of experience in slumming in the East End.

These gatherings were held in a mission hall run by the Church of England at the end of our street. They were quite popular. It was here I imagined I first developed a flair for organisation plus a little aggressiveness tempered with persuasion. With my bright blue ribbon sash across my chest sitting at a table taking the kiddies' halfpennies, entering this on cards, reprimanding the noisy ones and generally trotting after Big Brother from Oxford, I must have felt somebody. My function was really to see that the kids kept quiet and obeyed orders from Big Brother. "Big Bonee" and "Crafty" were often hissed at me but I was capable of dealing with such insolence once I got the hissers out in the street. Punching kids on the nose I quickly learnt was not the best method of persuasion as I was very small for my age and the bigger boys could easily have made mincemeat of me. I threatened, therefore, that I would blot their copy book when the annual outing to Epping Forest came around. This annual treat, the only outing in the year when, as a child, I was able to see the open country, was given to us free by the church people to all total abstainers under 12 years old. We had a long ride in four-horse brakes, a free tea of bread and strawberry jam and dollops of seedy fruit cakes. What we couldn't eat at the time we secreted in our pockets, which crumbled long before we got into the horse brakes to come home. Bad manners, of course, but what do half-starved kids care about etiquette? The church effort was a valuable one because it got the children young enough to learn the lesson about the evils of over-indulgence in alcohol.

As I have already indicated, the London Fire Brigade of my childhood had a fascination and a romantic image for me and my generation. I can still see those two grey horses standing patiently in their stalls at the fire station, their heads facing the open doorway, harness over head ready to drop on to their backs at the pull of a rope.

The interior of the fire station had its glistening steel pole down which slithered the men from their quarters above and the rows of pegs on which hung their brass helmets and steel hatchets. The double folded doors were painted a brilliant red and were flung open wide on the sound of the alarm. The engines themselves were pictures of polished brass, coils of white hosepipes, numberless brass taps and gadgets on which much bull or elbow grease must have been spent.

Let the alarm sound and where, at one moment, there was complete silence there came the sound of opening doors, bells ringing and harnesses jingling. The opening of those big doors signified to the passerby that a free spectacle was afoot. From nowhere it would seem a crowd would collect to witness the start of the chariot race. If we were privileged to witness the two minute scene inside those doors, we would observe the drill and efficiency of it all, but then the doors would swing back, the fire bell would start clanging, the horses given their lead and away they would go like fury, all street traffic giving the right of way when they heard the bell. The spectators viewed it all with excited admiration.

Chapter 4

Mother Trotter had been married twice. Her large brood was referred to as a menagerie. The wonder of wonders was that she and her 14 children had survived the perils of childbirth and infancy without the aid of a skilled midwife. Her children were a tough lot who grew up, married and produced families of their own. There was the resulting chaos of nephews and nieces as old as uncles and aunts with whom they played. It was all rather confusing. Where they all slept was also a puzzle but then a number of other families were also packed like sardines into those four room cottages.

As Mrs Trotter gave birth to her daughters the question of naming was promptly and easily settled. They were to bear the names of flowers, taken from a nurseryman's catalogue — Poppy, May, Lily, Primrose. Her sons should have biblical names — Thomas, John, Peter and so on. (When children enquired where they came from, our parents told us that the doctor had brought us in a black bag, and it was further explained that the doctor went into the country and picked babies off gooseberry bushes and handed them to fathers coming home from work.)

Mother Trotter was most successful in getting all her girls married off when they were comparatively young. Boys from other streets were always around and were not discouraged by a match-making mother who saw to it that the mates' intentions were most honourable. Otherwise, like an experienced matron she would, as she put it, "soon put arsenic in his honey pot" and sent the unwanted Casanova packing.

It was a customary cockney trait to bestow nicknames on most neighbours and no one took offence. Schoolboys especially practised it. My school nickname was "Jack" but it was dropped soon after I had left school at 14. Usually nicknames followed the pattern emphasising some physical or mental peculiarity not always complimentary. Constant use blunted any umbrage. When, therefore, Mr Evans came to live amongst us he was nicknamed "Tity Eye" on account of a cyst near one of his eyes.

Most wives, I suppose, like a handyman for a husband but in Tity Eye's case he was too handy and not efficient. In his spare time he would start on several jobs and never finish one completely. He started to decorate his front room by tearing down all the accumulated layers of wallpaper thus revealing cracks and holes in the plaster walls. He pasted over the cracks with pages torn from copies of the *War Cry* — and there he left the job. Visitors to his front room found themselves reading the writing on the wall — "A Drunkard Finds Glory!", "Twenty Sinners Seek Salvation!", "Seek the Lord and Be Saved!".

Tom Banks was a fussy man, abrupt in his manner and dealings and was not therefore popular with his neighbours as he did not drink alcohol and never visited a public house. His outstanding peculiarity was a slavish worship of his wife, Mary. Her state of health was his obsession. True, she was a frail creature, small and very meek whereas her husband was tall, full of bustle and consequence, a minor official in the government service somewhere. When out shopping together, they looked rather a curious pair — he so tall resembling a big alsatian dog and she toddling along by his side like a little poodle.

Being obsessed with the idea that his wife was a sick woman he had taken her to every doctor in the area for treatment. She must have swallowed a great deal of physic and pills, derived no benefit but had not come to any harm either. Finally Tom Banks found a specialist who said he could find nothing organically wrong with the lady. He suggested that perhaps a little exercise in the open air might improve matters and also suggested in a diplomatic way that if his wife got down on her hands and knees and did a bit of scrubbing her health would gradually improve.

Tom Banks went blind two years before he died and his wife had to help him. She outlived him by 10 years, rarely needed any physic and could be seen trotting around the market places doing her shopping as nimble as any little poodle out for a walk.

Jock Anderson said he came from Glasgow. No one knew his exact age or antecendents. Thus it was he was marked down either as a foundling or his past was a bit murky and therefore no one bothered about the details. One gathered from the neighbour with whom he lodged that he was a respectable bachelor, a non-smoker, a total abstainer, thrifty, hardworking and "cranky" on religion. He paid his rent promptly and that was a blessing. Most probably he had modelled his life on the self-help precepts of Samuel Smiles. Jock's regular habit every morning on entering the workshop of his firm was to light his bench gas fire and place upon it his tin can of "burgoo" or oatmeal gruel for breakfast.

The workmen often had breaks for talk and drinks of smuggled beer. There were no breaks for Jock or idle chatter: there was money in those piecework orders. But this devotee of work had to answer the calls of nature and even this had to be shortened in time by manipulating his buttons both before and after such an event. On his religious activities he apparently had gathered round him a small coterie of disciples, who met regularly on Sundays at various houses of the brethren to pray, testify, meditate and take tea. It appears one of their tenets was the right use of charity. For this purpose each member kept a "giving away purse" to which he had agreed to contribute a fixed sum each week. Jock was seen once placing money in two purses after he had received his wages. Asked why this procedure Jock said that one (displaying a little calico bag with a string loop) "is my giving away purse". "Who do you give it to?", asked his workmate. "Never you mind, laddie", he replied. "Where, how and who is my business".

Jock Anderson must have been getting well past 70 and his employers thought the time opportune for him to retire on a small pension. They hinted that much to him. But Jock was taking no hints so the manager had to bide his time and think of some other plan rather than upset an old employee. The opportunity occurred when Jock came back to work after being away for a short time with a cold. The manager called him into the office and said: "Well Mr. Anderson, I'm glad to see you well again. Now you must take things easy. At your age you should have a break now and again. We will keep the bench open for you, as we value you as an old servant. Just come in when you feel like it and leave when you like. We will dispense with the clocking in arrangements". Jock went back to his bench highly delighted.

A fortnight after this interview the manager received a visit from the resident timekeeper on the gate. "About this old man, Anderson, sir, he's getting a bit of a nuisance: says you told him he needn't clock in and come and leave any time he likes". "That's right, Bates, I did tell him that; he's been ill and he is an old servant so we like to be lenient".

"Yes, sir, I understand all that", came the reply, "but he's knocking on the gate before seven o'clock every morning and we don't start until eight".

Little Tich Jacobs, who was born and lived in our street, was a perfect dwarf. He never grew beyond the 36 inch mark. To their credit, his parents never cashed in on their son's diminutive figure, although they received offers for him to go into show business. It was as well for I felt sure that if he had been exploited in that way, he would not have survived away from the protective care of his mother. Conversely, he was his mother's shield when she needed one most. Little Tich was an intelligent individual, getting a little pompous as he got older, but it added to his personality and to the gaiety of life in our street. About his dress he was very particular. A martinet at his job, his employers were a photographic firm, who engaged him as a timekeeper as well as a checker of loads coming in and going out in the days of horse-drawn wagons. Little Tich, it was noticed, possessed an outsize pocket watch and chain which he displayed in his waistcoat. When distinguished visitors were around the factory, Tich was for ever consulting his timepiece, obviously to impress visitors.

His employers were proud of him and had made for him a special stool and desk and seated there with pen behind his ear was the monarch of all he surveyed across the company's yard. So we had the sight of Tich trotting across the yard directing big burly carmen with their bigger horses and large wagons where they must load and unload their goods.

Little Tich shone best perhaps as an amateur football and cricket referee because he knew all the rules of the game. If he did not stand higher than a cricket bat the batsmen and fielders soon found out it was no part of the game to belittle the umpire. On the football field, usually Hackney Marshes, the visiting team were inclined to joke about the ref the home side had produced out of the hat. The visitors very soon learnt that he knew the rules and the tricks. We amateur footballers presented Tich with a silver whistle of which he was very proud for his services. Whenever photographs of the team were being taken we always placed Tich in the centre of the back row perched on hidden boxes. When the photographs were developed, Tich could be seen holding the lapel of his coat, his whistle proudly displayed.

I noticed, too, Tich's concern for his mother when she went on the booze. His agitation and concern going round to all the public houses to find her was real and pathetic. He died of anaemia at the age of 36 and was buried in a coffin made for a child.

Chapter 5

In my childhood I recall the enthusiasm, rejoicings, flag waving, patriotic fervour and drunkenness that swept through North Street, as indeed it did throughout the whole country, when war was declared upon the Boer Republic. I was, of course, too young at the age of ten to understand the politics and intrigues and the scandals of the whole sordid business. I gathered, however, sufficient information from the talks of my father that the nation was divided about the aims and objects of the war. Father was against the war and was, therefore, dubbed a pro-Boer. Due to the fact he was popular with his neighbours and a good "mixer", we escaped having our house windows broken and other vandalism, which is what frequently happened to other people considered to be pro-Boers.

This war was thousands of miles away. It was a golden opportunity for the armament trade and the service contractors and relieved somewhat the unemployment situation. The stay-at-home patriots indulged in hysterical and drunken behaviour, often getting out of hand when celebrating "our victories". Father told me it was Lloyd George who lost his trousers at a meeting in Birmingham trying to speak against the war. He only escaped the hostile attentions of the crowd by departing down the back stairs of the hall disguised as a policeman.

Naturally we children were all for the celebrations. We played games like "English versus Boers", wore celluloid buttons in our lapels portraying our favourite generals like Buller, White, Baden Powell and Lord Roberts. It only required the relief of Ladysmith or Mafeking to set the whole populance dancing, singing, waving flags, getting drunk and finishing off the celebrations with bonfires and fireworks. Mafeking for all I and other children knew might have been in Timbuctoo. But on Mafeking night Joe Franklin, the landlord of the "Bakers Arms" public house, in our street, sold or gave away many barrels of beer. Nearly everyone was gloriously drunk. They let off a lot of fireworks and in their drunken frenzy tore down the wooden shutters from the cottages, which had stood the test of over 60 years, to make a huge bonfire in the street. We children enjoyed it immensely especially as the fire brigade was called out to save the cottages from going up in flames too. In South Africa soldiers and volunteers were dying from wounds, neglect and sheer incompetence.

Father would be sitting in his sacred arm chair in the corner of the kitchen, airing his views about the "Billy Muggins" who thought the war was being fought in defence of our "glorious Empire" when it was nothing but the annexation of South Africa for exploitation by mine-owning companies. "How much of the Empire do these cockneys think they own I should like to know?" asked my father. "Not one of them in this street own as much as a flower pot of earth in their own back yards, even the price of a pint of beer sometimes".

Father was contemptuous of his own class at times, always complaining about their apathy and ignorance of politics and religion. When he came back from the City of London on one occasion he said he saw top-hatted gentlemen on top of horse buses blowing tin trumpets and saving Union Jacks as an example of celebrating one of "our victories". It was all so silly and much of it spurious. "When the war ends," said father, repeating himself for the umpteenth time, "how many of those volunteer soldiers if they are lucky to come back alive will be out of work, some nursing their wounds on pitiful pensions. They will be pawning their medals and selling matches in the gutter for a living". My father was right because I lived to see it happen.

In the East End we had our own Boer War hero. His mother lived "up the top" of our street. When our hero Jock Sutherland came home to stay with his widowed mother I marvelled at his kilt as he belonged to some Scottish regiment. He was a fine figure of a man and considered the street's pin-up boy. It was on the occasion when his kilt was seen hanging on the backyard line to dry that I had misgivings. To my young mind it did not seem right and proper for a grown man to go about wearing short frocks.

Not all our street neighbours were true cockneys. We had many residents who were Irish, a few Welsh and some born in Scotland, who had been assimilated into our community life.

I remember too, we had no Jews or "foreigners" living among us. They would have had a rough reception and their life mad a misery had they attempted to live in "our street".

An example comes to mind of an old Jewish gentleman, doubtless a rabbi, living in a large house in Gore Road, Victoria Park (a middle-class area then) which was near to North Street. We children nicknamed him "The Holy Kicker". Why I don't know but no boy could pass this old man's house without kicking on his door, ringing his bell, throwing stones at his gate and occasionally breaking his windows. Why did we do this? It had become a ritual. There was no rhyme or reason for it except he was a Jew and they had invaded the East End as had other races in the past and were exploited by their compatriots, cheapening their labour products to the detriment of the East End English cabinet makers. As employers of labour they were ready to exploit this new penniless immigrant labour which the government did little to control.

Our local public house, "The Bakers Arms", was one of the focal points of this anti-alien agitation, largely because it was in the district and home of numerous small furniture makers. These were the survivors of the old garret masters written about by Henry Mayhew in his *London Labour and the London Poor* (1862). This small furniture trade had become particularly affected by the cheap, shoddy treacle polish products then being turned out by the many sweat shops in the area. The tailoring, garment and rag trade was also affected by this cut-throat competition emanating from these domestic room-cum-machine shops.

My own father-in-law Wells, who was one of these furniture masters, thought there was a need for regulation and control. Basically he had no objection to a person's skin colour, creed or nationality. To talk to him about the brotherhood of man and the granting of asylum to the oppressed as a noble ideal was one thing. When you come to experience, as he and others did, that your standard of living was menaced and pride in your craft going down the drain because of this unregulated influx of penniless people, who were being exploited, this was quite another thing, which no professional body of people would tolerate.

So self-contained was that North Street community (and this applied to other East End streets too) that even after 60 years, I was able to recall most of the names of neighbours and the men's occupations. There were 53 names — the occupations were: eight cabinet makers, two builders and decorators, four book binders, one painter and decorator, four builders labourers, three carmen, two engineers, one coalman, five shopkeepers, one postman, one quill pen cutter, three glassblowers, two clerks, three laundry workers, one book marbler, one seaman, one time-keeper, and two army pensioners. The rest were labourers and jacks of any trade.

At the end of that dingy street of ours was a more middle-class dignified property erected about the time Victoria Park was established about 1845 and named Gore Road. The park came about when Parliament decided to sell York House for £72,000 and provide a Royal park with the proceeds in honour of Queen Victoria. The land thus purchased had an acreage of about 200 acres and then comprised brickfields, market gardens and farmlands. It was in Gore Road that the family of William Booth of the Salvation Army came to live with his daughters, and they used to pass through North Street to get the tramcar to Whitechapel. Gore Road had substantial houses inhabited by middle-class folk. Some of these houses had basement areas for servants and tradesmen entrances with wide stone steps to the front door for the upper class. Charwomen cleaned those steps once a week and charged threepence.

In some of those basement kitchens would be the receiving end of a speaking tube through which the master or mistress from the rooms above would give their orders to the staff. Some of the houses had a series of bells suspended from the kitchen ceiling either numbered or named. These bells were connected by wire to the overhead rooms, a tinkle on any one indicating to the servant that someone required attendance. One of my reactions as a boy when I saw all those bells and wires was to think how pleasant it would be when I grew up and became rich, to lie in bed and pull on bell ropes instead of having to turn out at 5.30 on a cold, wet, freezing morning to put cans of milk underneath those stone steps. The dream never materialised.

Mr Rooney was one of our neighbours who came from Ireland. His forebears must have kept pigs and poultry in and around their hovel in a remote corner of his native land. He continued the family habit in our street, with fowls roosting in his kitchen. His few fowls roamed the street for neighbours' scraps. I never saw Rooney or his wife feed the birds with any grain. When Mickey Rooney hinted at keeping a pig in his backyard, neighbours roared their disapproval. All Mickey said in reply was: "Ah, sure there's no need to get aeriated about it — I was only making a suggestion". His back yard was stacked with wooden boxes of all sizes. He was a street hawker of fruit and vegetables sold from a two wheel costermonger's barrow which he trundled around the East End. When not in use the barrow was dismantled and the parts stored in the "parlour". It never struck Mickey's imagination to get rid of his pile of boxes. It would have to collapse from sheer size before he would do anything about it. When he was not too drunk he would struggle to climb to the top of the pile of boxes and, fortified with a can of beer and a tin whistle, he would entertain all his neighbours, whether they liked it or not, with renderings of Irish melodies. For a change he would burst into song, usually those lamenting leaving "auld Oirland" and wanting to return to native shores. This the neighbours devoutly wished he would do. After a little liquid stimulant he would launch into shouting challenges to anyone who could prove he was not a good Irishman. As no one appeared to trail their coat over his boxes, he would then shout: "Am I a liar?" There was no answer. He would answer himself: "No! I'm a good Irishman". Having satisfied himself he would continue his performance of tin whistling, serenading and challenging until he either fell asleep or, more often than not, fell off his pile of boxes to be later dragged indoors by his wife, assisted by her copper stick if he declined.

Father believed in Home Rule. "It's worth it", he would say "if only for one simple reason: it might give us natives a bit of sleep some nights".

We had two other characters for neighbours, Mother Burney and Mrs O'Keefe. They were married to two Irish retired soldiers, who were living somehow on small pensions. They were companions, drunk or sober. Mother named them "the Kilkenny Cats". Both liked gin, and they could only get the spirit in large doses at the end of each month when their husbands drew their pensions.

As a boy I earned many a halfpenny from Mother Burney who did a little secret drinking and who employed me to purchase her half quarter of gin, costing 2½d. Like mother's sister, Alice, her stratagem was to meet me outside her street door, await my return and I had then to smuggle the small bottle of stuff under her capacious apron. Both these Irish women smoked clay pipes. Sometime, about their husbands' pension time, the pair would go out together on a 'spree', visiting a number of public houses, get well and truly drunk and finish up having a row, otherwise called a "shindy". The flow of abuse and bad language was equal to anything that came first hand out of Billingsgate Fish Market. It was not an edifying spectacle in public but it was a lurid diversion in their dull and dreary existence, cooped up in their bed sitters.

One den of iniquity and a deprived area was the Jago area behind Shoreditch Church which was immortalised in Arthur Morrison's book *Child of the Jago.* This area was put out of bounds to me by my parents but I defied that restriction once, and I found the area cordoned off because of an outbreak of smallpox or cholera, so I quickly decamped and said nothing.

Pockets of skulduggery existed all over London in my early years. Hoxton was another and this was also out of bounds for me. In that area I recall a policeman was garotted and after that policemen went about in pairs at night. My wife's uncle was a victim one night when he was carrying home money from the club of which he was secretary.

Yet, outside these areas of evil repute, apart from drinking and gambling, the local people were friendly and not addicted to crime. My own street, for instance, was a case in point. Joe Blanders was one of our neighbours. He was small in stature, very pompous in his official uniform and peaked cap as he walked around a number of East End streets crying: "Dust ma'am, Dust toi". He was employed by the local borough council to do just this. No one saw him do anything else except drink beer. He thought himself a town crier and, therefore, with tradition behind him became very pompous. But the irony of the situation was that, in the presence of his wife, he was far from that. He showed obvious signs of being badly hen-pecked. His wife ruled him, figuratively and literally, with a rod of iron. Joe was wayward in his habits once he had got the "sherbert fever" (otherwise taste for beer) so when he was drunk he invariably started to put on the heroic attitude. "Dutch courage" we called it and it was not fair to the Dutch. During this "heroic" episode of Joe Blanders, high words could be heard coming from his home. Presently out would come Joe chased by his wife brandishing her iron kitchen poker. She would be bellowing a string of abuse but, being rather stout, she had to give up the chase. Joe would then go off and sleep ''rough'' for a few days, usually in the workshop of his father-in-law who had been, in his time, a borough councillor and instrumental in ''pulling strings'' to get Joe his job as a ''Dust-toi'' servant of the council.

Householders were expected, when hearing the cry in their street ''Dust-toi'', to put out their dustbins — if they had any — or prepare their passageway for the smelly carriers of dirt and germs to pass through with wicker baskets. These the dustmen would fill up from the pile of rubbish in the yard, carry the muck through the room and tip it into their cart. Contractors sometimes did this job and, be it noted, all dustmen wore their own clothes, not even overalls.

When Joe had ''knocked up'' a sufficient number of houses, he was left with ample time for leisure and refreshment, which was spent around various public houses, which in those days were open for the most part of the day. Beer was cheap at two pence a pint. One could get drunk on a shilling — ifyou had one.

Bill Quicksley was our next door neighbour, a printer by trade. Only occasionally did he go on the bottle but was one of those people who should never touch alcoholic beverages. In times he would follow his hobby of photography. His backyard was stacked with quite a number of small cases full of glass plates; the celluloid film had not yet arrived. I well remember those plates of glass for quite another reason than holding them up to the light to see the pictures. His children and myself abstracted a few plates at times, placed them at the far end of his backyard and pelted them, through a pea shooter, with pellets of putty. A ''hit'' or a ''crack'' or a ''smash'' would entitle the shooter to so many cigarette cards from his opponent.

About this time cigarette cards were becoming popular with children. We pestered the life out of passers-by for them. Playing cards in the street meant that they got in a filthy condition and must have been a positive menace to a child's health but we were not to know that, raking, as we did, amongst the muck, soot, road dust, horse dung and flies that littered our street gutters.

Personal hygiene was not practised as a habit: it was performed in fits and starts. It must be said for most mothers, however, that they had a great love for soap, soda and hard scrubbing. Carbolic they found very useful to keep down the smell from the drains; its antiseptic qualities were incidental and not a relevant reason for its use. I remember street hawkers came round the streets selling the stuff in pennyworths; we provided our own bottles. For some time this favourite fluid of Lord Lister's was also a favourite with the suicidel cases, who found it cheap

— but a horrible means of taking a short cut to end it all.

But to come back to our neighbour Quicksley. He would go berserk after a drinking bout. He would smash everything in the house unless our elders forcibly restrained him by tying him up with rope and allowing him to sleep the effects off. I was terribly frightened of him and thought of him only as a raving lunatic. During his spells of temper, his wife and children would take refuge in our cottage. The final episode in his life was played out one day when he came home fighting drunk and smashed every pane of glass in his cottage with his bare fists. His hands and arms copiously bleeding, he disappeared into the night. The police dragged the canal near our home next day and recovered his body to which he had tied several bricks to make sure of his intentions.

Chapter 6

During my boyhood there was a great effort by the churches throughout the East End to recruit youngsters into the Band of Hope to inculcate ideas of temperance. For boys especially there were also efforts to form companies of the Boys' Brigade. Baden Powell had yet to emerge from the Boer War to launch his Boy Scout movement. The Boys' Brigade was nothing more than dressing up boys in army-type uniforms, drilling, marching and carrying wooden rifles, blowing bugles, banging drums or organising drum and fife bands.

This endeavour by the church to recruit youngsters into semi-military organisations caught on for a time with those of our street and the surrounding area. We all flocked to join, including myself. But the enthusiasm was shortlived. It died from its own exuberance. On the opening night, the local mission hall was crowded with boys, short, tall, thin and fat, ragged as well as a few smartly dressed, all eager to put on a pill-box hat and a canvas belt with brass buckles, ready and prepared to shoulder a wooden rifle. Unfortunately, there was not enough equipment to go round, which caused a great deal of dissatisfaction. A boy without a pill-box hat and other accessories felt naked and ashamed to go marching and drilling. The two missionaries in charge of enrolment were overwhelmed with paper work. The upshot of that opening night was that every boy disregarded orders and words of command. They formed themselves into groups and marched round the hall singing all the popular music hall ditties with appropriate cockney wording and ribald phrasing unbecoming for a church hall. Their repertoire included *The British Grenadiers* to the words with which every school teacher of boys was conversant but which were unprintable. This was hardly what the missionaries had in mind and the lady at the small organ did her best to render *Onward Christian Soldiers* fortissimo, without success.

My father held iconoclastic views about religion and was of the opinion that the cockney (someone born within the sound of Bow Bells in Cheapside — and my father was born in Norwich) was not necessarily anti-church. The cockney used the church for all ceremonious occasions such as birth, marriage and burial; otherwise he was indifferent to religious practices and left them to the educated class in society. This type passed through North Street (usually in the middle of the street, not on the pavement) in their high hats, frock coats and their womenfolk overdressed in fine clothes. A working man in his Sunday best suit hobnobbing with the gentry was unthinkable. The front row pews or selected seats were bought and sold for a fee and an appropriate label attached to the seat and ''sidesmen'' appointed to shepherd the customers to their seats.

The clergy, as educated men from the universities, were treated by the cockney with respect and deference but it was not lost upon the cockney that they bought and sold their livings like so many pork butchers who bought and sold their businesses.

There were among the professing and religious people a few characters and hypocrites. One such was known to my father who claimed he was the original of Charles Dickens' Mr Pecksniff. My father was, no doubt, wrong in his dating but in his description of one of his employers, a Mr Dale, the role of Pecksniff fitted exactly. He was a special example of the ''Piety and Business'' type. He would arrive each morning at 9 o'clock at his business premises in the City of London, complete in top hat, black kid gloves and a Bible under his arm — to be noted as a mark of piety.

On entering through the warehouse door, always opened ceremoniously by his foreman, an obsequious Uriah Heap-type of fellow, Mr Dale would walk to the centre of the factory floor. This was the signal for all work people to stop work and look solemn. He would take off his hat and gloves in an affected manner, hand these to his foreman, gaze around the factory walls and ceiling play acting, so father said, the ''man of God'' — ''how holy and righteous he must be''. The foreman would then place a small mat at his feet, upon which Mr Dale would kneel, open his Bible at any odd place and in a graveyard voice offer up a prayer for the souls of his staff and implore the help of the Lord to sustain him in the successful running of that day's business.

My father thought this was perfectly harmless. It pleased the boss and hurt no one except it was in bad taste and provoked the contempt of his work people. But the hollowness of it all was made manifest when, on occasions immediately after the prayers, the foreman would be summoned to his master's office and informed that there would be a reduction in some piecework prices or some other bit of screwing up affecting the workers' piecework rates. There would be no consultation about it; it was ''just see to it or get out''. It is no wonder then that all his work people, with the exception of Uriah, the foreman, were a scoffing, irreligious crowd once outside the premises. Father said often enough to me that religious humbugs like Mr Dale did more to drive people away from the Bible religion than all the rationalist literature that was ever printed.

In about 1902 there was a furore and riotous behaviour by some Hackney people, assisted by outside supporters when a reverend gentleman named Smyth Piggott, practising his brand of churchianity at the Agapemonite Church, Stamford Hill, announced himself as the second Christ. This was more than many local people could tolerate. They expressed their disapproval with curses and cobble stones outside his church and his nearby home. As a boy I had to go along to see the fun. It must be said that the New Messiah did not wait long enough at Stamford Hill for the scoffing, angry crowd to crucify him. He left his living to another religious body. With his wife Ruth and their child and members of his sect they departed to quieter quarters in the West Country. Obviously he was not prepared to suffer martyrdom. He was only a diversion, a five minute wonder, a religious megilomaniac — or was he a charlatan in a dog's collar? Who knows and who cares at this distance in time.

Soup kitchens were a real and necessary part of our East End life. They were a charitable effort on the part of religious bodies for the down and outs of the area. Even the rest of the East End community were not slow to avail themselves of the cheap soup sold in these halls and hired empty shops.

My mother often sent me to the various places where the soup was for sale at a penny a quart. There would be a long queue of adults and children carrying a varied assortment of utensils for taking home this wholesome food, consisting of scrags of meat, lentils, pea flour, carrots, celery and stock from butcher's bones. I recall filing through one mission hall off Russia Lane, Bethnal Green, a decrepit area, where the down and outs, tramps and such like, sat at rough wooden benches with their bowls of soup and lumps of bread and eating with obvious relish. Those people who stood in the queue paid a penny or tuppence for their soup, which was cooked in a huge brick copper situated at the end of the hall. The latter was enveloped in steam and pungent odours of the cooking which tantalised any hungry soul. At the side of the copper stood a matronly woman with a ladle for filling our jugs, basins, bowls and whatever other domestic ware mothers could find suitable for the purpose. In those soup kitchen days people had a reverence for bread. To throw away even a crust of stale bread was considered a sin. Remnants of bread were given either to the beggars or, what was usual in working-class families, mothers made scraps into bread puddings, adding a few currants.

It was the spectacle of such squalid and abject poverty as seen in the rags and haggard looks of those human castaways as they sat at their wooden benches that must have planted the seed in my mind which eventually grew to that big question troubling a number of adolescents of my age — Why? Why all this scraping the bottom of barrels, the queue for soup to feed the underdogs of our society when one could read about, if not see, the ostentatious display of wealth, the banquets of the rich? Why had all these poor wretches come to this place and still refused to go into the workhouse and hide their rags from the public gaze? Was it through their own folly and wickedness? Why were the rich class rich? Was it because they were good and virtuous?

These questions began to trouble me every time the picture of that hungry scene flashed across my young mind. There were times when economic conditions got so bad that missions would give the soup away free to all who cared to call. But you had to have a ticket. Sometimes a missioner gave them away at the school gates when we children were released from school at noon. There was no organisation about the business and consequently, there was a near riot every time the missioner was seen at the school gates. The boys literally mobbed the old man shouting and jostling each other for possession of a ticket. The old man wore very thick glasses, held aloft the tickets while he moved to and fro to hand them out. Whilst this scrummage was going on, he would carry on a running commentary, consisting of biblical texts, to which the boys were completely deaf. The mass of shouting and pushing boys were intent on obtaining one of his tickets or cuffing and pushing the boys in front of them. One of the texts, of which he kept reminding us was: "Remember Christ said: 'Suffer like children to come unto me for they shall not want'. Here's your ticket child".

As the lucky one tried to push his way out others tried to push their way in. Another of his sayings, as he pushed the boys around him, still holding his tickets aloft was: "Now if any of you want to be saved you will have to be washed in the blood of the lamb and that will absolve you from all sin". On each occasion he came round to the school he gave us some more evangelical talk but there was the same pushing and shouting. Whatever he said was literally and figuratively well over our juvenile heads. The old man showed missionary zeal and spirit, a wonderful faith and courage to come among such a howling mob of young Dervishes. I never entered into this free-for-all for as much as I tried to snatch a ticket for his mission's excellent soup I usually retired from the struggle with more kicks than tickets.

The depths of poverty were still with us 30 years after Dickens had died. I remember our workhouse fellows, out on a day's leave to find work, searching the gutters of the streets for castaway cigar butts and cigarette ends. They would take back whatever they found to their workhouse and trade the horrible stuff with fellow inmates.

We boys loved to run alongside the high-wheeled dogcarts. There was a competition to see who could keep pace for the longest time. The carts were driven by a dandy young man, and a Dalmatian dog (we called them "plum pudding dogs" because of their colouring) would run between the two wheels. It was while I used to indulge in this game with another friend, George Bee, that the driver (whom we nicknamed "the toff") would throw down his cigar butt. Such a prize was much appreciated by our fathers for their pipe smoking and it transcended all the glories of being the last boy to give up the race to be able to get the butt. It was when I was once running along with George that what was thrown down was no ordinary butt but a cigar of fair size and still alight. We settled that we should each have a few puffs at it. Not long after we both grew pale and were sick. After that I never smoked again until I was past 20 years of age.

When I was young most men smoked clay pipes as these were supplied free by publicans to their customers. They would usually buy cheap shag tobacco, costing a few pence an ounce. Some tobacconists allowed a customer to help himself to a handful of shag from a big jar on the counter. Cigarette smoking was a rarity for my father's generation. Packets of five cigarettes cost one or two pence and were sold to boys older than myself. We called them "coffin nails" or sometimes "gaspers". No "nice" woman smoked; only the "fast" types did so in public houses. Snuff taking was on the wane by that time. If snuff takers were questioned they always claimed that the habit kept the head clear and that they were free of colds. My mother was a secret snuff taker as the family did not approve of the habit. As she lived to be 88 one can deduce that if snuff taking didn't have any positive effects, it did not do her any harm.

Chapter 7

School held no terrors for me, but for others it had the tortures of of hell. Among the boys there were some who were crafty and played truant. The girls, however, took it out in howls, tears and temper. One girl in North Street, Minnie May, staged a caterwauling scene so often that it almost became a ritual. My mother called the child "the morning howler". Minnie's mother was equal in size and voice to any company sergeant major on drill parade. Mother May called her offspring all the abusive names she could think of, short of doubting her own marriage lines. The punishment that poor child received on her return from school would rival the horrors of the underworld. The diabolical threats were breathtaking — "I'll skin yer alive, yer little bugger"; "Let me git 'old of yer, an' I'll break every bloody bone in yer carcass"; "I'll wring yer bleedin' neck when yer comes 'ome, yer jes' wait."

With refractory boys things were different. Fathers sometimes took a hand and used a belt. More often mothers applied the cane and were usually effective. My father never laid a rough hand on his children. This was always left to mother and she kept a penny cane in the corner of the kitchen for the purpose.

What little corporal punishment was inflicted seemed to maintain discipline. One street boy I remember was a regular truant and he for a time became the boys' Robin Hood-type hero. He had left home to live rough and had built himself a shelter among the refuse of the council's depot yard off Graham Road, Hackney. The depot itself was a large one surrounded by a high wall, to which dump a few favoured boys were invited to take tea with this truant Diogenes. "Slomiky Bill", as we called him, had hidden himself away and fitted up shelves to hold a few utensils appropriated from the council's store. Tea was made in a beer can and was handed round in cracked cups. It seemed an adventurous sort of life but our romantic notions of Robin Hood and his Merry Men holding up Norman knights or relieving the barons of their gold and jewels vanished from our minds when we came up against the stark realities of this "dump". Slomiky Bill was nothing but a little sneak thief. In order to live he was robbing old women's shopping baskets of food and taking cans of milk from people's doorsteps. He finished his boyhood days in a reformatory. It was my first sight of a delinquent social misfit.

Another aspect of street life in my boyhood days was "gang warfare". Our opponents were the boys of Russia Lane, Bethnal Green, where there were several high tenement buildings. Such buildings were one of the early experiments by housing planners to keep slum dwellers vertically instead of horizontally. They also gained a higher rent roll that way. The tenement dwellers of Russia Lane had a bad name, being considered by outsiders a nest of thieves and low barrow boys, only once removed from hedge-hopping gipsies.

However, these street feuds started amongst the young, or what they were about, their real cause was obviously bad housing conditions, overcrowding, mass unemployment and all the rest of the evils surrounding East End life. Throwing stones was about as much as we kids indulged in and the police, once on the scene, who had roughly a two-hour beat to walk, soon put a stop to our boyish behaviour. It was considered foreign and not "sporty" to carry — let alone use — cycle chains, rubber coshes, guns or knives in any of our fights. Nearer 14 years of age, on leaving school, this gang warfare ceased to have any attraction. We began then the jobs of organising our own football and sports club, in an amateurish way to be sure but this directed and absorbed our interest.

The boxing fraternity in our midst used to arrange little private fights on Sunday mornings with public house betting on the contestants. Our street gang leader in this respect, Henry Bullen, was a big and hefty boy for his age and came from a family which loved prize fighting and boxing. He was in his 20s when a fight was arranged by two rival public house cronies for him on the banks of the Regents Canal. That particular Sunday morning gathering, with all the various backers on both sides present, proved to be his last. He must have received a blow near the heart which proved fatal. Such contests were, of course, secret and illegal but like street betting, pitch and toss and card gambling they went on just the same. If the police put in an unexpected appearance, every one suddenly went deaf, dumb, blind and silly.

For the first 14 years of my life I heard and spoke very little but cockney slang. But I then began to realise there was a different language between that in the books I read and the language of our teachers in the classroom and the language of the cockney street. It required a great effort and concentration to drop the accent and so on, on going out into the outside world. In moments of strain and excitement, it was easy to fall back into the old idiom of early speech.

I think I was nine years of age before I saw any real wide open country, smelt the tang of country air, the smell of hay making or witnessed flocks of sheep and herds of grazing cattle. I knew nothing of the wealth of nature, the life and pursuits of country people; it was a totally different world to me.

I knew all about cats and dogs. I even kept a tame white rat with pink eyes once but animals like cows, pigs, fowl and sheep were quite outside my experience beyond the fact that, occasionally, we had animal meat on the table to eat on Sundays. As for the fact that cows had to mate to produce a calf to enable mother to buy skilled milk at a penny a quart to me, this was a complete mystery. I didn't learn the real facts of life, strange as it may sound, until I was 14 years of age when I became aware of what was taking place in the animal world. Everyone around me thought it was indecent to teach or even to hint at the comparison between animals and humans.

The nearest approach to the country before I was nine was the banks of the River Lea at the bridge near Springhill, Clapton, and Hackney Marshes. The latter were then flat expanses of grassland, often flooded in the winter to relieve the pressure of water on the lower reaches before the water flowed into the Thames around Barking. In the summer the so-called back rivers flooded the River Lea and its many canals — and also took sewage and what else have you from the chemical, paint and soap works. It was a place where midges and mosquitoes bred in their millions and amused themselves in the evening driving pedestrians crazy with their attentions.

To walk the distance from my Cambridge Heath home to the River Lea or the marshes and back rivers was a long one for any boy. It could only be attempted during our school holidays with other adventurous boys. This meant going without a dinner at home and we dare not ask for sandwiches. We had a weary trudge homewards footsore and terribly hungry searching the gutters for apple cores and the like.

The fascination about these back rivers was that we could fish and bathe in the water without disturbance — it was a no man's land. Our parents forbade us to go near the place, with good reason, because of the danger to non-swimmers and the evil reputation it had. Those back rivers on Sundays were the haunt of gamblers, card players, and others playing pitch and toss free from the attention of police. We caught very few tiddlers and bathing in the doubtful purity of the waters we were not encumbered with bathing trunks, had no towels to dry ourselves so we ran about and let nature do the job. Of course, we arrived home tired and hungry and had to face up to a caning and were sent to bed. It made no difference. As each summer holiday came round the lure of the back rivers saw us venturesome boys deserting the bricks and mortar and chimney pots and we went back to nature regardless of the consequences.

I must have been very young but I remember a winter when the snow was so thick that neighbours had the whole of their front doors blocked with six feet of snow. They even had to cut a channel through the middle of the street to gain access to the main thoroughfare of Mare Street, Hackney. The ice on Victoria Park lake was so thick that father was able, with hundreds of other East Enders, to go skating. This skill he had learnt whilst working in Aberdeen, under contract for three years. From the safety margin of Victoria Park lake, I marvelled at his performances, doing figures of eight and other graceful performances. He talked also of his being able to skate on the River Lea from Clapton to Hoddesdon, Hertfordshire and back.

Many years of winter residence in the East End prompts me to assert that in my lifetime our winters have been gradually becoming less severe. Every family had pairs of steel skates when I was a boy as part of the furniture. I doubt very much if you would find one pair in 10,000 London homes today.

A well-established feature of Victorian life was the practical joker and we youngsters were never at a loss to follow in our parents' footsteps. In my innocence I was given a bottle and sent to the oil and colourman's shop and told to ask for a penn'orth of "strap oil". Another request was for "penn'orth of elbow grease and don't forget to ask to have it wrapped up in brown paper". I never liked the look in the shopkeeper's eye when he gave me a small parcel of axle cart grease, who said on handing it to me: "If you come here again for that stuff tell yer bruvver, I'll grease his arse with the stuff, d'yer see!"

There was a confection in sweet shops called hundreds and thousands. They were very small round sweet pellets of many colours. Innocents were sent to buy "a farthing's worth and pick 'em out all reds".

These small pellet sweets came in useful to our neighbours, the local glass blowers. By making a fluted hollow glass tube in the form of a walking stick and filling the hollow tube with these coloured pellets they would "raise the wind" (money) by raffling the sticks in East End public houses.

As boys our practical jokes got as far as tying with string two door knockers across the street then knocking on both doors and watching the frantic efforts of both householders trying to pull their doors open. We made ourselves scarce when the string broke. Then there were the decoy tea packets filled with rubbish and the coin with a hole in it tied up with black cotton and put in the pathway of old ladies who would find the tea and the coin very elusive when they stooped to pick the items up. Our nuisance value games were all practised within the confines of the street in which we lived.

About the colourful street markets of the East End the competition was intense from the rag bag of a man selling four-a-penny boot laces in the gutter to the smartly dressed salesman prancing up and down outside his tailor's shop button-holing passers-by to "come inside and be fitted with a brand new suit for thirty shillings".

On the other hand there were "the old gels" who stood in the gutter and from whom you could pick up bargains in secondhand clothing and underwear. The "old gels" were usually buxom women of the costermonger type. They stood in the gutter with piles of old clothing. turning over each garment to advertise their wares, and making a running commentary on each article as it was held up for inspection. There was no shouting, just casual remarks to the circle of women gathered about the seller. "'Ere yer are, dear," she would say "Wot yer say to this nice bit o' finery? Luv'ly petticoat — two bob — one and six? C'm on, then, [turning the article inside out] wot yer say? A bob. 'Ave-a look at it, dear." (A "bob" was a shilling or, today, 5p.)

The "old gel", with a keen and practised eye and an understanding of the crowd, would pass the garment to a potential customer. More often than not the "bargain" would be bought. As each article was picked up and remained unsold it would be placed on another pile by her side. This, in turn, would be turned over as other women came up to take the places of those who left. I never knew mother ever to possess a brand new garment or hat. All her clothing she purchased from these women and she thought highly of her "bargains".

These parcels of clothing were obtained by the "old gels" from various sources, but mainly from the auction sales of pawnbrokers' unredeemed pledges. The itinerant rag-and-bone man with his barrow would also collect from households a great many worn-out garments and scrap metal in return for which he would offer a toy balloon or a goldfish in a glass bowl or even a paper windmill. The extent of this trade in old clothing, old boots or old anything was fantastic. It perhaps reached its end when the old goods reached the Whitechapel area where I saw displayed in the street gutters on Sunday mornings the most worn-out coats and footwear imaginable. As little as tuppence (1p) would be asked for old boots largely to the down and outs, and the foreign seamen who frequented the markets. The depth of poverty has its price and such trade went on for many decades in spite of the Sunday observance laws.

On Saturday nights all tradesmen kept their shops open until midnight, including the stallholders. Butchers had a custom of hanging carcases of meat *outside* their shops exposed to all the dust and flies of the market and bellowed their lungs out describing their joints of meat for sale.

Mother came to the street markets in late evening in the hope she might succeed in buying a cheap joint. If unsuccessful, she would trot off on Sunday morning with a few of her neighbours to Bethnal Green Road or London Fields market and buy a few block ornaments, as this cheap meat was called. She and others would buy very cheaply the "left overs" from the Saturday trading as they lay exposed on the stalls to dust and flies. Refrigeration was unknown then. On her return mother would wash the block ornaments in a clean cloth dipped in vinegar. But despite conditions none of us had food poisoning. Our "respectable" neighbours frowned upon this habit of Sunday shopping as they considered it ''very common'' and unChristian but mother's answer was: ''When the devil drives you must take care''. Father said it was bad management but who was he to talk as he often kept my mother waiting on Saturdays with the housekeeping money, haggling with her over a few shillings? Such tardiness in parting with the housekeeping money he never displayed when it came to treating his pals in the public bar, a common habit which lead to a great deal of unnecessary drinking.

Chapter 8

Child labour has now gone but in my young days it was an accepted thing. The money coming into our home was insufficient for the family's needs or so I thought and without any pressure from my parents I was prepared to do part-time work while at school. Circumstances at home were very strained. We had difficulty in paying the rent and the broker's men had been bought off temporarily on several occasions. I would go back to school at midday with perhaps only a slice of bread and jam for my dinner and would wait for mother to come home from her daily wash tub job at the laundry before we could get a meal. More often than not it would be a meat faggot and a dollop of pease pudding. It was as well that I was full of confidence in my ability to tackle any job that came along as otherwise the market for boy labour being plentiful and cheap I may have been discouraged.

In 1902, I heard through the school grapevine that the number five milkman at Warner's Yard, near Cambridge Heath, wanted a barrow boy. It was unnecessary to know his name. You just went along to Warner's Yard, asked for number five. If he wanted you, he told you to be outside the yard at 6 am next morning.

In Warner's Yard a dozen barrows could be seen looking as alike as peas in a pod. They stood outside a long, low brick outhouse. From the open doors and windows, clouds of steam were issuing. A great deal of noise was going on too, the rattling of metal cans, shouting and singing. My attention, however, was taken up by hearing the mooing of cows in a shed nearby. I looked through the shed's doorway and made a wonderful discovery. Tied up in their stalls were three live cows. They were kept in the heart of the East End especially for the sale of "invalid's milk", delivered in brand new cans at extra cost. The colour of this particular milk was much whiter than the usual delivery milk from the country via the railway, the latter having a slightly yellow colour and labelled "full cream", a statement accepted by all customers in all innocence and who would look with suspicion on milk up from the country? Dairymen of those early days were in no hurry to kill a deception which enabled the unscrupulous to skim a little more cream from their milk "just up from the country". Those who sold eggs encouraged the illusion that brown shell eggs were more nourishing than white shell eggs and a few unscrupulous ones tinted the white shells in tea or coffee and got away with the small increase in price.

By the time my eyes had become accustomed to the gloomy interior of the shed, I heard a gruff voice near me say: "Wot d'yer want, Nosey

Parker?''. I looked up at the cowman and saw he wore for an apron a dirty piece of sacking, greasy with use and an equally greasy old cap perched sideways on his head showing obvious signs of continuous pressure on the cow's flanks. The smell of cow's muck pervaded his person. He was chewing tobacco and spitting the juice all over the place. Putting on a bold front, I said: ''I want to see number five, please''. He looked at me and grinned: ''Yer do, do yer?'' Taking the lump of tobacco from his cheek, he spouted across the yard: ''Miller, Samson's 'ere to see yer''. No one heard his cry so he proceeded to the door of the barrow shed while I danced attendance upon him. He bellowed through the doorway, ''Miller 'ere's Samson, 'e wants to see yer''. The noise of clattering milk cans ceased and all eyes were upon me. There was a chorus: ''Miller, 'ere's Samson to see yer''. I looked through the clouds of steam and could see the dim outlines of men stooping over wooden tubs, washing milk cans and boys placing the cans on wooden racks to drain and finally loading them on to milk barrows ready for the next day's delivery of milk. When Joe Miller of number five barrow saw me he came forward and said: ''So yer want a job 'eh?''. ''Yes sir'' I answered. ''But yer a bit small, ain't yer?'' he queried. ''I can do the work, sir and I'm an early riser''. ''Orrite, be outside the yard six o'clock sharp tomorrow morning,'' he said.

I did my best. I helped to push that heavily laden barrow. I carried cans of milk to the various doorsteps as directed, hanging the cans by their handles on nails and hooks away from the attention of stray cats and dogs. The hours were long. I worked seven days a week and was engaged on an average 40 hours a week for 3/6 per week before and after school hours. Delivery of milk in metals cans in the 1900s was before sterilisation and refrigeration and mainly delivered to customers of the professional and middle class homes. Other people bought their milk from the roundsman travelling through the streets on regular ''beats'', usually three times a day. All the customers thought fresh milk was being served, yet really it was from the first consignment of milk arriving in London by train in the early hours of the morning. Roundsmen started the round about 6am and finished their work about 5 pm, Sundays around 2 pm. Although I kept my job for nearly two years I sometimes experienced great fatigue, dropping off to sleep about 3 o'clock on Sundays and sleeping round the clock until five o'clock the next morning.

On Saturdays between the three rounds I was engaged in polishing up the brass-covered milk churns and barrow with brick dust and lemon. It became a habit with me to get up at about five o'clock and spend 15 minutes in the local coffee house (advertised as ''a good pull-up for carmen''), swallowing a cup of hot tea and a slice of bread and dripping. The carmen usually breakfasted on tea, bread, kippers, bloaters or sausages before taking out their horses and carts for their daily work.

On Sunday mornings I got into the habit of closely looking around the streets for the odd chance of picking up an article of interest left behind by the odd drunk on a Saturday night. Oddments were many and varied. One drunk had turned out his pockets of silver coins and had taken the trouble of laying them out in a row along the kerb edge. They ranged from a five shilling piece to a threepenny bit, which was very thoughtful of him. I also found in a doorway of a factory what I thought was a gold ring which bore no hallmark. Mother promptly settled its fate by taking it to "Uncle" Henry, her pawnbroker friend, who said it was "Irish". Its nationality didn't bother mother and she pawned it for £3 which set straight family affairs for more than a week.

Drunks on Saturday nights were a common sight. Some had the benevolent spirit and laid in the gutter to sleep it off. There were others who were violent and wanted to prove it by giving the police trouble and having to be laid out on a stretcher — a body-length barrow on two wheels — and being wheeled off to the police station to the delight of all the boys following along hoping the fellow would burst his straps and put up a fight. The result the next day in court might be a fine or a month in prison to cool down.

Chapter 9

In 1904, my last year at the Mowlem Street Elementary School, my seventh standard teacher, Mr Barratt, whom we all admired, refused permission for me to sit the London County Council's Merit Certificate examination. He said that I had no time to do my homework satisfactorily because of my part-time work as a milk boy. This certificate, it was drummed into us, was necessary in order to obtain a worthwhile situation.

I overcame my teacher's objections by promising to find time. In our kitchen, shared by other members of my family, I managed to secure a corner of the kitchen table to work algebraic equations, do arithmetic and attempt mensuration problems; I discovered the longest rivers in the world, the names of the capitals of different countries; I learnt about our kings and queens.

On examination day, tense and apprehensive, we were marched into the hall to sit at special tables while the teachers, looking solemn and impressive, walked up and down handing out and receiving examination papers. I succeeded with distinction in geography, history, drawing and English composition. I received my certificate through the penny post. It was printed in black letters within a border of ash leaves, also heavily outlined in black. When framed it looked more like an outsized memoriam card. As a work of art it would have made William Morris turn in his grave; it disgusted all my friends and I was ashamed of it, too. Father said that it wasn't worth the price of a toffee apple when it came to getting a job, and as a reward for my labours it was a very poor return. Father called it a "pinchpenny bit of council cardboard." I think that he was right.

Mowlem Street School was a big brick structure, built in about 1875, and like most Victorian buildings it was built to last. It was divided to accommodate on three floors children under seven, boys and girls, with the latter assigned to the top floor and doing most of the stair climbing. The boys' rooms were divided into seven classrooms, and our classes were then known as "standards".

My class had a monitor chosen by the teacher, mainly because he came to school well dressed and wore a clean collar. I was never a monitor. His function was to help teacher but the class looked upon him as a "toady". Most scholars, as we were called, wore nonedescript clothing. It was the tradesmen's sons who were dressed in suits. Many boys, like myself, wore knickerbocker suits, made up from father's cut down trousers. Some had patches sewn on their backsides of different coloured material. No boy was self-conscious about this as it was fairly common. Most of us wore celluloid collars from white to yellow with age and use, likewise with their shirts.

The playground, in which stood the privies open to the sky, was suitable for about 50 boys to play in with comfort but usually held twice that number — a place for bedlam and noise. Really the 15 minutes break, usually called playtime, was given up largely to horseplay; organised play was out of the question. A couple of teachers walked around like wardens in a prison, ready to pounce on "bullies" and "all-in wrestlers". There were "cap fights", when we hit one another with our headwear, "riders and horses", or a set piece between "Boers and English". When the whistle blew we all had to cease shouting and talking and immediately stand to attention like statues. At a second blast on the whistle we fell into pre-ordered lines and marched upstairs. There, perhaps, we began our parsing and analysing of the English grammar, learning suffixes, prefixes, substantive nouns and subjective moods.

My passion for attending school was recognised by the London School Board presenting me and other like-minded scholars with reward cards, as they were called. They might perhaps seem a little dull and academic to any East End boy. For example, my brother William's cards from 1880 to 1890 included not only English but also Latin and French quotations, something of a farce to a working class boy who could hardly speak his native tongue correctly. The school board no doubt had every intention of implanting knowledge but they ignored that the seed was sown on very stony ground.

There was nothing new in this idea for reward cards were in circulation in various day schools as far back as 1860. My own dated back to 1894 and when I left school in 1904 I had collected 24. The first depicted English birds and their eggs, without any explanation; the remainder showed English wild flowers and places of national interest with information. My father had attended the Dove Row Shaftesbury Ragged School, in Haggerston, and he had 21 cards (1860-1870) which were all coloured and represented traditional national characters and costumes. But after I had left the school the parsimonious London County Council, which had taken over the running of London's school system when the school board was abolished in 1902, did away with the cards on the grounds of economy.

Perhaps it is worth my mentioning here that when father went to the Ragged School his parents paid 6d a week for him to learn his three "Rs"! He obtained a certificate from the great Lord Shaftesbury himself and was given 7s 6d for being "a diligent apprentice". Father thought little of the certificate which I found in his "dirty Dick's" cupboard when he died. I remembered that he resented patronage and charity from the leisured classes and in particular he disliked the word ''ragged''. ''We boys may have come from poor families'', he used to say ''but many of us were not ragged''. They had no desks at which to sit. They stood with a piece of slate and a rag for a wiper, and the headmaster was free with his cane to maaintain discipline.

But to return to my school days, at this elementary school in Bethnal Green (and repeated throughout the country in similar schools in similar places) only one pupil in 400 each year passed to a foundation or a grammar school, and this was 30 years after the provision of universal compulsory education! For the unlucky 399 it was just a free-for-all on leaving school at 14. There was the search for work, and it largely depended on chance whether a boy became an apprentice for a skilled job, or an errand boy, a can carrier for workmen or a van boy on the back of a horse-and-cart. Mostly they were blind alley jobs: the boy was sacked as soon as he reached an age to justify paying him higher wages. Many finished up as labourers, more often out of work, or as dockers standing idly at the dock gates like so many slaves in the market place waiting to be bought.

My school and street chum George Birch won a scholarship to the Parmiters Foundation School but because his elder sister had already won a scholarship the father said he could not afford to keep two children at school. George, therefore, at 14 got a job in a printers' works making tea and running shop errands and taking copy from printer to customer. He eventually emigrated to Canada and its gain was this country's loss.

What was I going to do then? ''Anything you like,'' my father said, when I appealed to him for guidance, ''so long as you bring some money home to keep yourself''. Father had long lost any ambition by following his dying trade of cutting quill pens.

Mother preserved my school report for 1903. There were 58 scholars in standard 6 and I was rated 14. I was ''very good'' at scripture, history, handwriting and composition, but the report said I was also ''very good'' at needlework. That decided mother who now said: ''From now on, son, you are quite capable of sewing on your own buttons.'' And I have done ever since.

Discipline was maintained by our male teachers with a generous use of the cane. The only exception was Mr Barratt, a rare specimen of his time, who preferred to maintain discipline — and succeeded — by methods other than caning. He refused playtime periods and set homework for breaking rules, and suchlike penalties. One of the ''rewards'' withheld was attendance at the public baths for swimming lessons. Since I never qualified for these, I and others were left to learn the art as best we could by paying many visits during school holidays to the Victoria Park lake. I did this unknown to my mother who thought that the lake water was dangerous if swallowed. As the lake had not been cleaned out within living memory she had grounds for fear. I do know the lake was full of "tiddlers" or small fish and scum drifted on the surface. It was George Lansbury, MP for Poplar, an area near the park, who was instrumental, when he became a cabinet minister many years later, in having it cleaned up.

My love for schooling must have been intense when I recall that, for seven years, I was never late or absent once. Every year I received a medal and the seventh was considered a "gold" one. Between the various "standards" there was a keen competition to maintain a high average attendance to gain the "school banner", which was bound up with a government grant, I believe. I remember the time when, playing football in the street, cobbled with small granite chips, I fell and injured my knee cap severely. The hospital doctor said that I had to be away from school for at least two weeks to rest the leg. Mother viewed that prospect with alarm. A note was sent to school and the outcome — my classmates arranged a rota of boys for two weeks to carry me "pick-a-back" to and from school rather than the attendance record should suffer. For two weeks I was hero number one.

The school must have had a devoted band of teachers because each year a festival prize-giving show was organised. The teachers spent a great deal of their spare time coaching the bright boys to sing, recite, start a minstrel troupe and perform a comedy sketch. To this show our parents were invited.

The infants from six to eight years of age gave a maypole dance on the village green which we made. It gave me the greatest thrill witnessing these youngsters in fancy dress winding in and out around the pole with their coloured ribbons to form a pattern. Local councillors and the mayor, in his robes and chain of office, were invited and the mayor would present the medals and prizes, make a speech praising the scholars, the teachers, the parents and Uncle Tom Cobbleigh and all, especially the parents (the voters) who had produced such fine children, who would be the future citizens and inheritors of this great and glorious empire of ours.

After I had left school the reactionary London County Council put a stop to the giving of medals and prizes and with it too went the yearly festival: all in the name of economy. Instead the same body was very patriotic and voted £8,500 of the ratepayers' money to buy flagstaffs so that each school in London and the scholars could salute the Union Jack on Empire Day. At the same time they denied to children a free meal if they were in need. "Patriotism up the pole," father called it.

The greatest benefit I received from my schooling was not so much vocational or academic knowledge but that it taught me to have a set of ideals and to strive to live up to them. This I suppose is what one calls "character". Whether this was due to the discipline of the elementary school or the methods of instruction by our teacher, Mr Barratt. I do not know, but he certainly taught me to go out into the world prepared to stand on my own two feet and face the obstacles.

The opportunities for reading books were extremely limited in our house. The kitchen table was constantly in use, washing was on the line overhead and the three chairs were usually occupied. I came to realise, after reading about the landscapes contrived by Capability Brown, that "you had to look at the prospect expansively".

At school for culture we were taught to read one of Shakespeare's plays each year and to memorise and recite particular extracts. Portia's speech at Antonia's trial was one I recall. Unfortunately for Shakespeare our teacher, Mr Barratt, was an enthusiastic and devoted fanatic of the Bard's work so that our class of 50 boys, versed only in cockney, began to hate Shapespeare and all his works. Mr Barratt tried to quicken our interest by taking us to a hall in Bethnal Green where some cultural folks put on the *Merchant of Venice* for our benefit. I liked it very much but I fear, at that stage of our mental development and half empty bellies, it was like introducing culture to children who cared more for Dick Turpin and Buffalo Bill than Shylock seeking revenge. Many of my class mates had an appetite for adventure stories and we formed a small club.

Our pocket money was meagre — about one penny a week from parents, plus a few coppers earned running errands for neighbours, holding horses or fetching cans of beer for neighbours from the local public houses. But, all the same, we boys managed to buy our "penny bloods" — comics — and swopped them. Such periodicals were condemned by our teachers (all from middle-class backgrounds) who would confiscate them. Stories about Dick Turpin, Robin Hood, tales of blood and thunder, held sway, as well as stories of Robinson Crusoe, and Scott's novels. *The Last of the Mohicans* and *Coral Island* were my favourites. Once a fortnight all the clever boys in the class had the first pick of story books so that the backward ones had to wait in anticipation for the current favourites. My enthusiasm for reading any and everything that came my way, be they "penny bloods" or more serious books, brought me into conflict with my parents who thought it bad for my eyes. The "penny bloods" were set up in small type, and, in those days of paraffin lamps and naked gas jets, my parents naturally tried to curb my reading. I read under the bedclothes at night, with the aid of a lighted candle, but my parents were right about my eyes for by the time I was 17 I was compelled to wear spectacles, having, so the optician said, "spoiled a good pair of eyes by overstrain".

Looking back at the literature I enjoyed at school, I remember that for the last hour at school on Fridays our teacher read to us from the *Brer Rabbit* threepenny series of stories. These enthralled us but the book which I treasured at the time was Mark Twain's *Adventures of Tom Sawyer.*

Chapter 10

Among the slums of the East End, in its mean and drab little streets, backyards and alleyways, built in an era of speculative and unregulated building, there were the public houses. They became hives of drinking and beer swilling, and they occupied a predominant place in the cockneys' life.

The public house was the hub of their social life and activities; the bars were constructed as cubicles designed only to stand up in, except for a few forms and empty, up-turned beer barrels to stand glasses on; the floors were covered either with sand or sawdust; the saloon bar was reserved for the richer clients and boasted chairs, a few carpets and spittoons.

A labourer in corduroy trousers, cap and a red handkerchief round his neck, would have been given marching orders had he dared to step into the saloon bar to order a drink. The saloon bar had small swivel windows erected on the bar counter, intended to hide the saloon customers from those customers in the public bar. Mechanics would use the private bar,-priced accordingly. The public house lavatories were usually off the premises, stinking places generally. Brewers were always going to "improve" their houses and never did unless forced by the licensing justices.

The social work of the church, judged in relation to the distress and poverty around it, was inevitably limited and touched only the fringe of a great problem. It largely consisted of soup kitchens for the very dregs and down and outs of the area. The churches had long lost their initiative and influence, if ever they possessed any amongst the mass of cockneys. Their approach to the problem of excessive drinking and the use of the public house as a social centre was fundamentally wrong. Where the clergy were mistaken, recruited as it was from the leisured class, was in its approach to most forms of public entertainment, Sunday sport and amusement — music halls as the work of the devil, a perverted view that drinking alcohol was the cause of poverty. It ignored the economic factor that, if all men kept sober, there would still be 10 men competing for five jobs in a capitalist economy. The established Church missed out the cardinal factor that what the cockney craved in his drab and miserable surroundings, and alternate periods of toil and idleness was entertainment and decent housing. All the church was offering was church services, choirs, praying and much ritual. The Band of Hope, with its condemnation of "strong drink", was restricted to children who regularly attended church and said their catechism. The same restriction applied to joining the Boys' Brigade.

The Salvation Army did, however, present a paradox. Their blood and thunder crusade against the Devil lurking around every public house bar did not prevent the "soldiers" and "lasses" visiting the bars to sell their *War Cry.* In another way the Army was realistic and not averse to attaching business to its religion, as witnessed in its workshops, farms for the unemployed, lodging houses for the homeless and so on. It was far seeing enough to exploit the possibilities of the bioscope, when it came along, in entertaining the East End youth.

When about this time, many mission halls were being sold to private concerns to be used for the new silent moving pictures, the Army used its own Congress Hall at Clapton on Saturday nights for cinema shows. For fourpence or sixpence, the crowd saw all the early Western cowboy pictures, were served with tea and cake, band music, hymns, stamping of feet and clapping of hands. Those who came a little late were placed behind the curtain and thus saw pictures in reverse but this never bothered them.

Any person in those early days with a spare hall, barn or shed could exploit this medium of entertainment. Whether the buildings were fireproof, overcrowded or had proper fire exits and appliances mattered little. We had to experience a few disastrous fires and loss of life before adequate regulations were introduced, fortunately not at Congress Hall. We youngsters packed the place on Saturday nights.

One of the many activities and features of some public houses was their occasional Saturday night concerts in a fairly large room. They were organised by the local fraternity on contemporary music hall lines in aid of a member in straitened circumstances. They had their jovial chairman and club artists as singers and entertainers, rendering all the favourite songs in which the audience could join in the choruses (helped by the penny song sheets sold in the streets of those times by hawkers). All who went were intent upon enjoying themselves, to drink, to sing, to clap and forget for the time being where the next week's rent was coming from. Some occasions would be benefit nights intended to gather funds to help a neighbour who had experienced some illness and financial misfortune. My grandfather, George Southgate, had such a night at the "King's Arms", Pritchard Road, off the Hackney Road, on 17 April 1886. It was billed as "a Grand Concert and Draw on behalf of Mr Southgate, Senior who has been laid up for some considerable time and unable to follow his employment. He, having lost his wife, stands greatly in need of your assistance. During the evening the following Articles will be disposed of by way of chance. 1st Prize Handsome Chiffonier full size. 2nd Prize Pair of Vases. 3rd Prize Set of Brushes. 4th Prize a Handsome Whip. 5th Prize Fancy Rabbit. Tickets 6d each."

The sentiment expressed in that sixpenny ticket, the friendly helping hand and the prizes pay eloquent tribute to the big-hearted cockney. His help saved my grandfather from finishing his life in the workhouse, the fate of so many old people in those days.

On the outskirts of Victoria Park, after its public dedication, a new type of public house, with large gardens, began to be built. Mine host put on garden parties during the summer. The trees and shrubs were festooned with little coloured glass lamps for such events in which burnt a small candle. There would be music and dancing, truly a revolution from the old type of small, beer-swilling bars. One such public house was the ''Sir John Cass'' in Victoria Park Road, the garden of which backed on to our yards in North Street. To walk along a high brick wall of nearly 16 feet was no obstacle to adventurous boys. We enjoyed a free entertainment, risking our limbs, provided we had the nerve to sustain us.

Some public houses put on supper nights, where there were gigantic joints of roast beef or pork, suckling pigs, trotters, tripe and cowheel with suitable vegetables. The local baker did the cooking and customers went round with a small cart to pick up the cooked joints to where customers were assembled making merry with the drinks.

There was one particular supper night at the ''Bakers Arms'' where Nobby Clark officiated as head waiter, potman, barman and chucker-out. Nobby was also a bookmaker's tout, taking bets on the side; he did a bit of boxing and otherwise kept himself out of mischief inspecting the pub's cellar as a ''bunger up of bungholes''. His pet aversion was a customer named Mad Jack Myers who, when he was drunk, made himself a confounded nuisance, especially to Nobby Clark. It was Nobby's job to throw Mad Jack out when he got to this stage. But Mad Jack was an elusive customer. For as soon as he saw Nobby approaching with tense jaws and an evil glint in his eye, Mad Jack would slip out of the bar door and slip into one of the other cubicles. These cubicles brewers called bars — jug, private, lounge, public or saloon — which they kept shut with a shot bolt. Customers sensing fun freed all the bolts watching Mad Jack popping in and out making faces at Nobby until he caught ''that bastard'' Mad Jack and flung him into the street. Next day Mad Jack would be sporting a black beauty, apologising that he must have slipped on some orange peel.

However, on this particular supper night my father remembered ''suckling pigs'' were the principal item on the menu. The guests turned up, and the tables were laid and looked fine with table linen, glasses, flowers and cutlery. The club turns were there, too, and all waited but no suckling pigs arrived. The landlord eventually rose from his chair and with an air of solemnity, announced: ''With regret I have to inform you that the suckling pigs have been stolen from Ross the baker''. This episode turned out to be the work of practical jokers.

Most East End public houses ran loan clubs, Christmas clubs, beanfeast clubs, and so on. By paying small sums into a common fund there was an eventual share out around Christmas. Some clubs were efficiently and honestly managed and some would run successfully for a time and then, when the day came for the share out, there would be the usual crop of defaulting officials who had absconded. In one case over £85 was involved — a lot of money in those days — for the usual reasons — gambling and backing slow horses.

Joe Franklin of the ''Bakers Arms'' public house was, in my boyish eyes, a wealthy man. He undoubtedly combined business with patriotism at the time of the Boer War. On every conceivable occasion when a ''victory'', spurious or not, was announced in the Jingo press he would call for a public house celebration. Joe Franklin was a small man with a capacious belly across which was hung a large gold chain. He sported a horsy necktie, studded with a diamond horseshoe pin. His fingers displayed gold rings and altogether he advertised wealth, made out of selling beer. He was generous to us school children, giving us toys at Christmas and an annual day's horse brake outing to High Beech in Epping Forest and a high tea.

The public house served excellently as a regular place of call for the street barrel organ grinders, and performers on tin whistles, violin, cornet and other musical instruments with or without vocal efforts. The performers would pay a round of visits to the various public bars with their begging bags. The barrel organ tunes provided an opportunity for young girls to learn and show off their dance steps. The public house of the East End was also the happy hunting ground of pedlars — some of them blind and selling boot laces, matches, collar studs — anything, in fact, to gain a copper coin as it was against the law to beg.

During those days factories and glass works employed boys with long poles studded with nails carrying beer cans from factory to public house for the men's beer. Tea was substituted at a much later time. Glass blowers were a very thirsty crew and their boy passed our door regularly each day on this errand. To interfere with that boy on his walk back and forth was considered a major crime, as one boy found out once for dropping stones in the men's beer cans. ''Taking the can back'' has been a common saying for a very long time, but it literally happened to me as a boy when I was sent to the local public house with sevenpence to be spent on bread and cheese (2d), pint of beer (2d), ounce of tobacco (2d), and a beer can on loan (1d). A box of lucifers and a clay pipe were free. When I took the can back the penny was mine for the task. All the cans were embossed with the name of the public house.

Chapter 11

The pawnshop was a part of our lives. Some people pawned their clothes, chattels and finery quite openly, others did so secretly with a sense of shame. To such people poverty was almost a crime fostered by the smug and leisured classes. It was endorsed by our prison population who, in their paradoxical way, committed a crime to escape a crime.

As I got a little older I saw no reason for feeling ashamed of being poor. Like Dr Johnson I felt sorry I was poor and even humiliated when I knew my Sunday suit was pawned to pay for the household requirements. Mother was an adept at pawning, though she did not always do it on her own account. She undertook commissions for others who thought poverty a crime and shuddered if other people should find out. Mother often said on entering the shop displaying three brass balls that the sign represented "Faith, Hope and Charity" but she had her doubts about the charity bit when she started bargaining with "Henry, our uncle". There was, though, an element of hope. On Saturdays mother would redeem the pledges. The secret pawners would pay visits to our home and ask mother to appraise the value of the articles shown before she spoke to Henry. She would review the various garments laid out on the table folding and arranging them in her expert way so that Henry could not spot the darns or frayed edges as he quickly ran his eagle eye over the article before him. If it was a small piece of jewellery mother and the owner would argue as if a duchess's diamond tiara was being popped. Perhaps the article would only fetch a few shillings but nevertheless, in those far off days, every sixpence was of importance to those to whom it was paid. For the task of pledging, bargaining and redeeming mother would receive a small fee. People liked my mother because she had the gift of hearing all, seeing all and saying nothing to outsiders.

When it came to sickness in any of the neighbour's homes, sitting with a dying person, a confinement (qualified midwives were too expensive in the East End) and even laying out a corpse, mother was equal to the task. What you did not ask her for was money. Of that, she said, she was always "short". She had a wonderful fund of good sense and anecdotes born of long experience. She was a born cockney, who could barely read or write but assumed she could, such being the lack of education of most working girls of her generation. She was employed on a sewing machine at the age of 12 and never went to school.

From various hiding places in the home, usually the big vases on her front room mantelpiece, she would bring out on Saturdays a crop of pawn tickets. As soon as I could read it was my job (taken over from my elder sister) to read these tickets over to her. ''Suit popped Monday 10,'' I would call out, holding a small ticket. ''Ah, yes that's Mrs Baxter's, that must come out'', mother would respond. ''Ladies shoes Wednesday 2s.6d.!''. ''Yes, that's Mrs Young, put that aside, she hasn't given me her money yet''. And so it would go on until she had what she wanted. I would then total the amounts pledged, make a rough calculation as to charges for ''hanging up garments'' or ''delayed payments'', then off mother would go with myself sometimes in attendance to ''Uncle Henry'' and redeem the pledges.

''Uncle Henry's'' pawnshop had a front shop window display of unredeemed pledges of countless articles useful or ornamental in all stages of wear and tear. A passageway through the shop led to four small cubicles with doors, all being served by one long counter. It was full of bustle, especially on Mondays (rent day), and there was a hum of conversation. There was a shout for Henry, and a call of ''I'm next'', and Henry saying: ''How much?'' as he opened the parcel before him. He viewed the contents quickly. ''Five shillings,'' came the reply. ''No, too much. Four shillings''. ''Make it four and six, don't be too hard,'' would be the retort. While Henry re-wrapped the parcel and threw it the length of the shop counter to a boy at the other end and amongst the racking and would start to call out the particulars of the parcel to his ticket clerk and pay over the money. This would go on all day if necessary.

One of the features of most East End streets of the 1890s was the little general shop. There neighbours could obtain mostly their domestic goods and food in what father called '''ap'orths and penn'orths'' — soap, bread, tea, sugar, bacon, margarine, carbolic, jam, paraffin oil; it was all there, stacked away on shelves, packets, tins, sacks, boxes and hanging on strings from the ceiling. Sugar lay in open sacks, tea in open chests, articles of domestic hardware, cards of pills for all common ailments. If anything had to be weighed, the shopkeeper would hold scales aloft and watch the needle. Scrubbing brushes hobnobbed with frying pans; broomheads had a nodding acquaintance with hams on the counter; and there was a wooden barrel of pickled herrings near common soda in sacks and sweets in jars. The bull head tin opener was for sale ready to open sardine tins, salmon and corned beef. During the summer months, amongst this conglomeration of goods, suspended from the ceiling sticky fly papers wrought devastation among the fly population. Outside the shop the flies were attracted by the aroma of horse droppings.

These little general shops were never erected specially for trading.

They just happened to fill a need and helped a shopkeeper to make a living. If any householder thought he or she would like to turn their front parlour into a shop there were no bye-laws against it and the landlord didn't mind as it meant an increased rent for him. In North Street we had six general shops and one public house for about 200 properties. In the 1870s there had been two public houses in the street but "The North Star" lost to its rival "The Bakers Arms". Only one thing remained to remind us of the departed and that was its large plate glass windows and a wooden cellar flap let into the pavement.

Mrs Dear who rented the premises ran a home wash laundry. It was her beer cellar flap that we children were interested in. We could never just walk over it for we had to jump on it to experience the bounce and noise. The home wash laundry deserves special mention because it was the means at times of saving us children going hungry on many occasions. Mother would sometimes put in a day's washing for Mrs Dear and thus kept our household in food when most in need. The laundry possessed one of those huge mangling machines operated manually by Mrs Dear's son, Eric. He hated the job as much as he hated school. It was his task to turn the handle and treadmill work it was. This enormous-looking mangle reminded me of the rack in the mediaeval past. There were two great wooden rollers weighted down at each end with iron weights. These rollers went backwards and forwards on flat beds of two inch thick mahogany, the propelling power being little Ernie who had to turn a great iron wheel nearly as big as himself. This wheel operated the rollers to which the clothes were fed by his mother. The work really was strenuous enough for a man to operate but the devil drives where needs must. The pay for a day at the washtub in my school days was around three shillings, and a meal was included.

Charwomen and washerwomen were amongst the lowest paid and considered the lowest in the status scale of domestic employment. There were more grades of service — and snobbery — in feeding and looking after the comforts of the professional and leisured classes than in any other trade or profession. Neither of my parents practised obsequious flattery or servility toward their employers. When I asked my mother why people looked down on washerwomen as being inferior, she said: "Because we can't help ourselves, son. We must wash their dirty linen and dirty floors in order to live. They are snobs and hold the money bags."

My father, too, would declaim on such matters from his armchair by the fireplace. There was his view on Tory misrule, his hero worship of Charles Bradlaugh the MP and self-proclaimed atheist and Gladstone, the Liberal leader, and his support of the economic theories of Henry George. That armchair was held sacred for my father's use and we children were not allowed to sit in it while he was home.

It was an ordinary Windsor chair, of the type turned out in their thousands and costing eight shillings paid weekly. Mother never paid cash for furniture for the good reason that she never had the cash to pay in full for anything in that line. This was no headache to her and I don't suppose she ever lost a wink of sleep over it. She never failed to honour her debts except that she would be tardy in paying instalments and clever in ''gaining time''. Sometimes I would be sent to the door when the ''tally man'' called to offer mother's excuses. Once I said to the caller: ''Mother is out!''. ''I know she isn't'', said the tallyman ''there's her bonnet hanging on the hook, see''. Mother could not resist this as she listened from the kitchen. She poked her head round the door and with her usual cockney repartee said: ''Oh! is it? I've a pair of drawers hanging on the line in the yard outside but that's not to say I haven't got a pair on''.

Father was once summoned to the county court over payments due on the chair. The registrar ordered a court payment of two shillings per month. The debt collecting firm could have taken the chair away (and kept the instalments) but they preferred a judgement summons. The debt collecting agency sent threatening letters on vivid blue paper. Mother tore them into narrow strips and she made pipe lights of them for father who blissfully used them unaware of what they were.

Chapter 12

"Mother's parlour", as we children affectionately called it, was our front room immediately entered from the street. At night it became a bedroom. An art pot holding the aspidistra stood on a table fronting the street window together with a Bible and a brassbound album of family portraits. The professional photographers of those days posed their subjects against the background of heavy furniture and curtains. Everyone was over-dressed in all their finery, looking sedate and commanding attention. The window of mother's parlour was draped with lace curtains doing their utmost to exclude daylight and the prying eyes of passersby. Chairbacks and the sofa had to be covered with antimacassars which were more ornamental than protection against the macassar hair oil, which some men used. Table legs were sometimes draped but this was, however, a protection against the family cat, Jim Ruff, rather than, as some moderns have asserted, an excess of prudery. The window sill outside the street window was scrupulously cleaned with hearthstone as was the front doorstep every Sunday morning.

Every woman prided herself on her parlour mantelpiece, also heavily draped with cloth pelmets and side curtains. Here were shown off her glass shades and lustres, wax fruits and china vases. Every effort was spent to exclude draughts, so doors and window frames were curtained. At night the window frame bolts were shot home and the outside wooden shutters were also bolted. This was done nightly together by laying the sausage-like stuffed rollers along where the top and bottom window frames met to exclude draughts. However, it also prevented fresh air from getting in and the smell of stuffiness and camphor balls from getting out.

When mother had disposed her furniture about the parlour — a six foot sofa, six chairs and two tables — there was just enough room to move sideways around the centre table. Providentially this table folded upon itself and was removed to the backyard when we had company on "concert nights". The mantelpiece, which father named "mother's altar piece" and which no-one was allowed to interfere with, kept company with the vases and tall oval glass shades, under which she kept the bridal ornaments of her once radiant girlhood.

Only on Sundays did we have a fire in the parlour grate. "Just to air the place" was the reason but we could never escape the odour of camphor, camphor balls hung above each picture frame as an antidote against mildew and bad smells. The purpose of "the airing" enabled the family to have a Sunday dinner together. We moved sideways round the table to our allotted chairs and there we had to stay until the person nearest the door moved away.

At the time of the Dublin Lockout, when there were many thousands of starving Irish families, my parents offered the use of that room as a committee room to raise funds on behalf of those people, and the street collectors from all over East London would come and go, with their coinboxes.

My father was stirred into action by the words of George Russell (A.E.), the poet and writer:

"Your insolence and ignorance of the rights conceded to workers universally in the modern world were incredible and as great as your inhumanity. If you had between you collectively a portion of human soul as large as a threepenny bit, you would have sat night and day with the representatives of your labour trying this and that solution of the trouble, mindful of the women and children who at least were innocent of wrong against you."

Few homes were without the family get together either on Saturday or Sunday. Thrown largely upon their own resources for entertainment and amusement, apart from the public house and music halls, relatives met regularly. In my boyhood there seemed never-ending gatherings at each other's houses of uncles, aunts and cousins. Children were relegated to the kitchen until required to say their party piece and given a clap and a piece of cake, for their effort. Beer flowed freely at twopence a pint, providing all the stimulus needed to dance and sing.

Pianos were not in vogue then in the East End but accordions, concertinas and mouth organs were. Both father and my brother William could play the English concertina; my grandfather too, who had his own music book.

My parents followed the accepted East End pattern, inviting friends and relations to our home for a sing song. They all sang the popular current music hall "hits" and all the old favourites of which they never tired. The golden rule at all such gatherings was that everyone had to do their best singing solo; no matter if we had heard the darn song a thousand times before no-one ever cribbed at hearing it again. Uncle Bill Yorston's favourite was:

"I've just wiped a tear from me eye
I've just spent the bob [one shilling]
They gave me for the job
And I'll meet 'im in the sweet bye and bye".

Mother gave us her two favourites *Annie Laurie* and *The Old Mill Stream.* Aunt Moggie sang *Maggie* and *Cows Being in the Clover,* the emphasis being on "Maggie" — an imitation of mother's long rendering of the name. The only song father knew was *Medicine Jack* (then over 50 years old), and the audience joined in a verse: "I'm a jolly old quack, quack, quack''. Father wore a battered high hat, carried a pail and a sack on his back, did slapstick stuff with old corsets and an assortment of ladies underwear, which never failed to raise a great deal of laughter and applause. It was all unsophisticated fun and they amused themselves.

The virtue of saving was always impressed upon us children by our parents but I never knew either of them to save a brass farthing to set us an example. Father's allowance to me as a schoolboy was a halfpenny a week, and increased to one penny providing I cleaned the knives and forks on Saturday and cleaned his boots on Sundays. There was no chromium plate and stainless steel cuttlery then and I had to use emery paper and brick dust on a board for cleaning. Higher up the social scale knife machines were used but they were beyond our parents' pockets. Whatever extra money we wanted had to be made by running errands for neighbours, sometimes laying and lighting fires for orthodox Jews. My sister had to hearthstone people's doorsteps. Our parents had no long stocking to dip into just for the asking. All that we earned was in return for services rendered. Men in their cups would be accosted by children saying: ''Only a farthing, sir'.'' The men would demand something tangible to justify his largesse, and any cockney kid would rise to the occasion either by doing a cartwheel, walking handbalance on the pavement or even show him a decorated grotto of shells and tinsel paper or a dressed-up ''guy''. Father's method was to insist that they all gathered round him in the street and sing their heads off. At the conclusion of this choral effort he would fling a handful of coppers in the air and cheer the children most heartedly as they scrambled and fought to pick up the coins. Sometimes he would make them run races in the street and for a time the street was alive with noise and excitement. Father was very popular with such children but mother, remembering her empty purse, would remind him that ''charity should begin at home''.

If there should be a horse brake outing to the country there were always boys prepared to follow the brake doing cartwheels and every so often calling upon the brake party to ''frow out yer mouldy coppers''.

My young sister Nell and I decided that all the coppers we earned running errands for neighbours should go into a money box marked: ''Country holiday''. I got a condensed milk can, slit up the edges and nailed them to the floor of my bedroom. The prizing of this fixed safe served its purpose. We had learned the lesson of self-help and the value of money for services rendered; and our parents respected our wishes. We shared the contents equally.

The Children's Country Holiday Fund enabled my sister and me to spend a fortnight in the real country to us, at Stock in Essex. I was then nine years of age. My first impression was the smell of country air as something quite distinct from the smoky dust laden air of Bethnal Green. Here in rural Essex I saw field upon field of meadowgrass, numberless wild flowers, sheep and cows grazing, fields of vegetables, apples growing on trees and acres of corn waving their heads in the breeze. It was all very strange and exciting to a child from another world. Another boy and I were taken to a cottage where the lady made us welcome immediately by putting before us hot dumplings soaked in beef fat. Her first injunctions, having been warned perhaps that we were wild savages from Borneo, were that we must *not* climb the fruit trees in her garden. It was about the first thing we did as soon as her back was turned and had the intense pleasure of seeing real red apples growing on trees. They were not ripe; we got a tummy ache and were sent to bed early for disobedience.

Christmas Day was a family affair and we sat down to a gigantic feast of roast fowl and mother's Christmas pudding which she boiled in the brick copper outside in the yard, the same copper used by father in which to harden his swan and goose feathers in hot sand before cutting them into pens. She continued to make smaller Christmas puddings each year for each of her children after they had left home and continued this yearly practice until she was well past her eightieth year. There was the custom of "Snap dragon" when the hot Christmas pudding was brought into the darkened room, placed before father, who would pour some brandy over it, set it alight and start to eat it to the shrieks of delight from his children. Like all other children we hung up our stockings for the presents from Santa Claus. There were not many and not expensive and throughout the rest of the year these were our only toys we had to play with. We were certainly not spoilt with toys and what we did have were simple things which we invested with a great deal of imagination.

(I remember only once being taken to the theatre to see a Christmas pantomime. It was *Cinderella* at the Britannia Music Hall, Hoxton. We were dressed in our best clothes and had to walk through a multitude of dingy streets like our own. We were given buns and sweets by some unknown benefactors and we shrieked with laughter, yelled our applause at the appropriate moment, marvelled at the glass coach and hurled curses at the ugly sisters. We sat enraptured at the transformation scene with its ever-changing coloured lights, the trap door act of the Lupino family and chasing of Harlequin by the clown, who had a string of sausages and a red hot poker and never once caught Harlequin. For a few hours we were transported into a fairy land of delightful dreams.)

That small front parlour also saw death. Once in the corner, against mother's mantelpiece, shielded by a dark grey blanket hung from a string across the room, lay a small elm coffin resting on trestles. In this coffin lay the body of my little sister, Florrie, aged nine. Relatives and neighbours came and went to gaze upon her little body as she lay in white calico sheets. They had come to pay their respects and to weep. One had to pass and re-pass through that parlour from the kitchen to the street so the presence of death in the semi-gloom was inescapable. There was the smell of flowers laying at the head of the coffin, the chrysanthemums especially, and that smell for years always reminded me of my childhood playmate. She was the same little sister who had taken me to school on my first day, who held my hand and kept reminding me on the way to be "a good boy". In this I miserably failed by setting a lucifer match alight in the classroom. She died when mother was out charing. I recall I crept up into mother's bedroom where Florrie lay crying and in pain. Her face was tear stained and its alabaster colour was heightened by her black raven locks. I climbed on to the bed to hug and comfort her until she fell asleep. The next thing I knew she was laying there in the coffin sleeping her last sleep with an angelic face and mother telling me, as a comforting thought, that her soul had gone to join the angels in heaven.

Chapter 13

Old graveyards seemed to me to be untidy places when I was a boy — weed ridden, looking more like a bankrupt stonemason's yard than fitting resting places for the dead. I remember the extensive graveyard surrounding St John's Church at Hackney. We played hide and seek amongst the grave memorials under which lay for a great many years the bones of hundreds of once prosperous citizens of the then village of Hackney. There were long rows of oblong brick-built vaults surrounded by six foot iron railings; all terribly neglected, iron rusting and bricks covered in lichen. In other parts of the graveyard there were hundreds of tombstones of all descriptions in all stages of decay, leaning at all angles.

One particular tombstone took the form of an oblong table with its four legs intact. Carved out at one end of the table top was a representation of four playing cards. Several legends surrounded this queer memorial and, as no adults cared to visit this neglected section, a few of us children, secure from the eyes of visitors, used to visit it and play around it. Father told me his version of the legend which we children accepted as gospel truth. A party of Hackney residents were assembled around a table in a friend's home playing cards for money stakes. One of the party was losing heavily. He became desperate and agitated. Unknown to the other players he was trying to recoup money he had taken from his employer's cash till. In his last throw, he excitedly exclaimed: "Strike me dead, if I don't win this". He lost, promptly collapsed and died. This so shook his friends that they turned religious, gave up card playing for money and erected this table memorial over his grave as a warning to all gamblers and users of profane language.

Table tombstone, along with all the other brick and stone memorials, has been removed and in its place the authorities have created a pleasant garden with seats just as my iconoclastic father had advocated many years before and for urging this, his mates said that he must be an infidel.

A familiar Hackney figure for a great many years when I was a boy was "Blind Jim". He could be seen on most days sitting on a stool placed on the pathway which went through the burial ground to and from the church. On his knees would be resting a large Bible in Braille. From this he would be reading continuously. His livelihood was entirely dependent on the offerings of passersby. Blind Jim symbolised for me an indictment of society which had little social conscience beyond private charity for the handicapped and afflicted. In my grandmother Southgate's large scrap book compiled by her about the 1840s, she had pasted an illustration of an old building depicting blind people engaged in weaving, cord spinning and basket making, with the printed caption: "Hospital and School for the Indigent Blind at Norwich", and I noted the word "indigent".

In my young days I often heard criticisms by blind people of institutions for them as little better than "sweat shops", however well intentioned the founders may have been. Begging was, therefore, a recognised form of "living" for such handicapped people but the law stipulated that the beggar must have something for sale, be it bootlaces, matches or some other trifling thing.

Funerals played an important part in the life of an East Ender. In particular the costermonger type excelled in putting on a lavish funeral display when one of their number died. They would beggar themselves in order to put on a "good show". The rest of the working class were not so extravagant but they also spent far more on funerals than was consistent with their means. In fact, all insurance money would be spent in this way. Relations had to be buried "decently" and "respectable" and not as a "pauper". If the deceased never made much of a shine amongst his friends and relatives, they were now going to put him first in the show and no one would then say a bad word about him. The tribute, therefore, had to be made with elaborate trappings and flowers.

My father used to call such funerals "blackberry beanfeasts", on account of the extraordinary black clothing that predominated plus, of course, the quantity of beer and gin consumed. The funeral cortège would halt at a public house on the way back from the cemetery for a "quick one". The journey was more or less a leisurely one in the days of horse-drawn carriages. A few rounds of drinks to speed the soul of the departed were called for, or so some mourners thought. The party would finish the evening with further drinking, some getting maudlin drunk, a few wanting a fight. Within a week it was all forgotten and the departed was just a memory. A great deal of money must have been spent on wreaths and flowers alone, and an extra carriage would sometimes be used to carry them. Neighbours made collections from door to door and in pubs where the deceased was known. "The empty chair" wreath was an eye catcher; an anchor-shaped wreath was for a sailor, then there were others depicting a barrow, a broken column or a harp with broken strings. The funeral procession would be diverted through several streets so that everyone would have the chance to pay their respects. Neighbours would close one of their wooden shutters or pull down the blinds; shopkeepers would tack a wooden board across their windows.

There was a great atmosphere surrounding funerals: two mutes stood at the front door of the dead person's house, while pallbearers, looking intensely solemn, wore polished hats with drooping black cloth attached to the hatband and bows outside. They carried in one hand a black rod with a polished brass band which was only discarded when they helped to carry the coffin. All mourners wore black. Handkerchiefs had deep black borders as did all envelopes and notepaper used for such occasions. Even bowler hats had the wide black cloth band, which was also worn on coat sleeves. Grief for the deceased had to be outwardly shown as well as inwardly borne. The widow would be overwhelmed in black. Her widow's veil hung over her black bonnet down to her waist. The funeral hearse displayed much polished brasswork; it had a slightly oval roof which was decked in ostrich plumes surrounded by a cut metal fringe. The hearse was drawn by four handsome black Spanish horses, ostrich plumes on their heads. Their sides draped with dark velvet cloths, which sometimes had different coloured cords and tassels, denoting the age and sex of the departed. Children under the age of one who died were buried in white coffins. Horses were trained to slow step, high step and toss their majestic heads as the cortège moved slowly along. The coffin, under a number of wreaths of flowers, was of highly polished elm, studded with ornamental brass handles, nails and plates.

Mare Street, Hackney, was in parts a very narrow thoroughfare when I was a boy, a survival of its once village days. Inset in the granite cobbled stone street was a single gauge tram line along which trundled a two-horse drawn tram car. To travel from Cambridge Heath to Stamford Hill or Liverpool Street Station cost tuppence. The pace was leisurely as the tram stopped to pick up or put down passengers at whatever spot they chose by pulling a bell rope, although agile men and youths jumped on and off the cars.

Most boys in those days scorned paying fares. The practice was to steal rides when the conductor was not looking. Other horse-drawn vehicles equally served the boys' purpose but that meant watching out for the driver's whip. This game was not without danger. I remember one serious accident when Bob Williams, a schoolmate, was riding behind a brewer's dray. A heavy ladder, which draymen used for unloading beer barrels, fell off and young Bob with it crushing a leg, which had to be amputated. If a tram conductor managed to snatch off your cap — and every boy wore them then — while taking these free rides he would make you run a considerable distance before he threw it away. To go home minus a cap meant a caning from mother, and there was no deceiving her as to what you had been doing.

Tram cars never turned round. The horses were unhitched, led to the other end and hitched up again for the return journey. The tops of the cars were uncovered, open to all weathers. In the winter the drivers needed to dress themselves to look like Arctic explorers.

Sometimes when I had finished school at four o'clock I had to take a parcel of father's quill pens to a firm of stationers in Panyer's Alley, off Paternoster Row in the City. He gave me tuppence for the journey from Bethnal Green Road. I managed to make the whole journey and back by free rides behind carts, taking short cuts through the maze of streets. The tuppence was spent on the way you may be sure but the journey was always an adventure trying out new ways of reaching my destination without losing myself in the City of London's streets and alleyways.

It was during one of these short cuts between Bethnal Green and Shoreditch that I was to witness the unusual sight of a small area of property cordoned off to traffic and pedestrians. Bales of straw were strewn about and notices displayed: "Danger". Police were on duty and I was warned about short cuts. Here was an outbreak of smallpox or some other infectious disease. The sight was sufficient to strike terror and panic in me after some of the stories told me by my elders. The place looked like a deserted village.

When the first motor buses with their solid tyres and heavy chassis rattled over the granite cobble stones, they made a fearful noise. If one broke down, as they often did in those early days, there was traffic chaos until it was dragged away amid the "chaff" from horse carmen and tram drivers. But they were the new form of public travelling which had come to stay.

There were very old houses and shops fronting the Narrow Way of Mare Street opposite the old Hackney Church tower then given up in their old age to such fleeting businesses as wax work shows and salacious picture machines offering the delights of "What the Butler Saw" and "A Night in Paris".

During my youth I was a regular visitor to the gallery of the Hackney Empire music hall on Monday nights for tuppence. Saturday nights saw several young bloods throwing their weight about and making themselves a confounded nuisance to the rest of the audience. The cry would go up: "Chuck 'em out!", and the attendants promptly did just that. The attendants were usually ex-prize fighters and kept an eagle eye on the front row of the gallery where occasionally a few youths would gather for the "pleasure" of dropping orange peel and other things on the heads of the people below. The attendants would pounce and the offenders would be bundled out neck and crop.

Monday was often a bad day for the halls and so one could get in the gallery for 2d or 3d, and from there I saw performances of all the great late Victorian and Edwardian artists — Marie Lloyd, Vesta Tilley, Dan Leno and Little Tich among them — though sometimes I would be perched up so high that down on the stage they looked like pygmies.

Andrew Carnegie, the American millionaire, provided funds for the Central Library, in Mare Street, Hackney. There was a row about it at the time. Those opposing his gift said that they didn't want his ''blood money'' wrung from the ''slave workers'' of his steel works in Pittsburg. But the ayes had it and I found the library very useful in those early days.

The Sunday custom of my childhood prohibited all kinds of games being played in the street. It was something enforced by all parents, although none of my neighbours were churchgoers. The main thoroughfares, however, on Sunday evenings became what we commonly called ''monkey parades'', when most East End youngsters dressed up in all their finery to walk up and down the thoroughfare, usually in pairs, like so many peacocks on the lawns. Occasionally, some became bold, exchanged pleasantries and then paired off, the boy usually buying his girlfriend some sweets, leading perhaps to a kiss and laughter at their boldness. This would be the first and perhaps the only introduction of boy meets girl, the whole procedure described as ''getting off the shelf''. It would be followed by a flirtation period and finally, if the two suited, ''going steady'', being introduced to one another's parents, and then marriage. A feature of those ''monkey parades'' I noted was that two young females who could afford it dressed exactly alike, style, materials, hats and accessories. A couple of ''Johnnies'' would also appear, similarly turned out, and playing concertinas. They handicapped their progress I thought by visiting public houses for stimulants arriving home tipsy and the worse for wear.

Couples were accepted into families only as courting and allowed to ''bill and coo'' in the front parlour on specified nights, ''love'' being taken as an accepted fact. The main consideration surrounding all such matches from the point of view of girls' parents was had the prospective husband a job to maintain a wife?

Parents' advice to their marrying children was brief, simple and blunt: ''You've made your bed, you must lay on it''. The newlyweds always tried to live near their old home surroundings and wife's mother's watchful eye. Help was always close at hand if wanted.

No one, male or female, appeared in public without a hat. Hatless males were considered ''cranks''. It was the age of the top hat (first class), bowler hat (second class), and cap and choker (third class). The public houses had bars which were used much in the same order and priced accordingly.

Womenfolk of the East End copied their wealthy

contemporaries in their dress habits — when they could afford it — excelling in voluminous dresses and picture hats, the latter contraptions of artificial flowers, birds, fruit, draped in nets and veils of diaphanous material. They also wore stiff corsets, laced up at the back, looking more upholstered than dressed, and petticoats. They wore high elastic spring-sided boots or boots with rows of ball buttons running high up to the calf and requiring a steel hook — and time — to button up.

Great-Granny Smith, on mother's side, was born during the time of the Napoleonic Wars. She was a big woman, wearing an enormous size bonnet, voluminous skirts, shawls and veils all decked out in black alpaca. She presented to me a formidable figure as she sat in that small parlour of ours dwarfing everything around her.

I recall no women smoking when I was young, neither did they use powder or make up, the answer being perhaps that they could not afford it. But had one done so she would have been dubbed a "tart" or "street walker" and we had none of that kind living among us. Our mothers may have been coarse and loose in their speech but in matters of sex they were censorious and never discussed it. As one old dear said to me once on this question: "Everybody knows, as they get older, that they are either a boy or a girl: no one has to tell us".

Chapter 14

About the time that the Hackney Music Hall was opened there still existed off the Hackney Road one of the last of the ''penny gaffs''. Mayhew describes them as existing in many parts of the metropolis in 1850. ''Penny gaffs'' had largely disappeared by the 1900s except ''The Belmonts'', known locally as ''The Flea Pit''. It maintained the tradition of such places right to the very end — colourful, noisy with melodrama and excitement.

''The Belmonts'' advertised itself by flashy posters put around the district. Inside the hall was very rough wooden seating, dim lighting by naked gas jets covered in a wire frame. There was singing (always with choruses in which the audience joined), jokes, coarse and otherwise, by the comedians and interjections from the audience, not always complimentary. Persistently noisy members of the audience were hustled out without ceremony by chuckers out. Adults were admitted for tuppence and juveniles one penny. If you ate oranges you threw the peel either on to the stage or at anyone in the audience you knew and this was treated as a friendly greeting — all part of the show.

My father put ''The Flea Pit'' out of bounds for me as being strong meat for one so young.

My brother, William, twice my age, defied the parental injunction and took me along once ''as part of my education'', he said. The memory of that visit had lived with me ever since. There was much pushing and shoving to get into the hall as there was no such thing in those days as orderly queues. It was everyone for himself. Whistling and shouting went on continuously while members of the audience inside clambered over the wooden benches to get as near the front stage as possible. The play, so my brother said, was an exciting one. It was all about race horses and stolen diamonds. There was going to be a real race horse on the stage — or so we were told.

As my brother had a passion then for a threepenny gamble with the local bookmaker, he thought I also would be interested, especially as nearly everyone around me talked racing and betting. The only horses around me were the cart and wagon-pulling type, except the occasional ''trotter'' of the ''dandy boys''. The play was set among stables and stalls with straw scattered over the stage. I saw jockeys walking about in gay colours and caps, slapping their riding boots with whips; there were ''toffs'', as we called them, because they wore top hats and smoked large cigars and ladies in frocks and frills handling sunshades, and wearing large picture hats with waxed fruits and bird wings. The whole scene was intended to portray Epsom Downs off the Hackney Road, leaving a great deal to the imagination. It had atmosphere — the horse even munching hay in its stall. There was banter from the audience about the horse, its starting price was lost upon me when the ''thoroughbred'' showed signs of nervousness although my brother assured me that all thoroughbreds were nervous creatures. But even he had doubts when I mentioned that the ''nag'' looked suspiciously like Bill Cronin's cart horse. He had to agree that this ''racer'' knew more about the cobblestones of Bethnal Green Road than the grass on Epsom Downs. Many fictitious bets were flying around among the audience as to the nag's chances in the Grand National. While all this banter and crossfire was going on the actors and actresses went on saying their lines, blissfully ignoring the betting odds hurled at them.

At the critical moment when the stable lad confronts the top-hatted villain caught in the horse stall, the owner of the fabulous diamond comes in. She turns out to be a beautiful girl, all curls and lace petticoats. She is in love with the stable boy but has never breathed a word about it. The boy goes up to the horse, lifts up one of its hind legs and discovers the stolen diamond neatly hidden in the horse's hoof. This is the dramatic moment for unmasking the thief and exposing him to the beautiful girl. The house was silent and intent, waiting for the beautiful girl's indictment of the top-hatted villain, when suddenly the horse excreted in full view of the audience. There was immediately a roar of laughter and applause, yells and advice as to what they could do with it, ''Put it on yer rhubarb'' being the most popular. As soon as the stage hand came in to clean up with pan and brush the air was rent with offers of ''penny a pail'', this being a cockney boy's effort to earn an honest penny from amateur gardeners.

As the old ''flea pit'' went out so the silent bioscope came in with a juvenile audience enjoying the blood letting, the shooting and thundering of horse hooves necessary in a Wild West film. There again the appropriate noises and tempo had to be supplied by a versatile pianist. This fellow sat in the wings playing the same tunes and making the same noises twice nightly, seven days a week.

Before the institution of the National Health Service medical practice in the East End of London could not have been a very lucrative one for a doctor. He was never called in to a case unless it was absolutely imperative because of the expense. His home visit was priced at half a crown and a visit to his surgery cost a shilling paid on the spot, a price which included a bottle of physic. Hospitals were run on voluntary contributions and charity bazaars. Admission to hospital was by a letter from a subscriber or the doctor. There were enquiries about means by the almoner, and while no one was turned away from the out-patients department, the waiting to be seen was long and tedious. People with all sorts of complaints mixed promiscuously in the large waiting rooms and corridors. It was not a pleasant sight to witness. They were usually the very poor with complaints due to neglect, poverty and ignorance of hygiene, and obvious VD and TB past any hope of a cure.

Doctors in the East End made their calls on bicycles, wearing frock coats and high hats. When it rained the doctor would ride his bicycle with one hand and hold an umbrella with the other. Of course, there were other doctors who could afford their own horse carriage and coachman. Consequently they charged higher fees but they were not to be seen visiting patients in our kind of neighbourhood. Mother's comment was: "Not for the likes of us; we can't afford it", but when the occasion arose (and patients had to be in a very bad way to necessitate a visit) there was a tremendous fuss in the home cleaning, polishing and preparing the patient and the room for the doctor's visit.

Due to the expense most parents avoided the doctor and therefore preferred to rely on a lot of old wives' remedies for both major and minor complaints. There was a long string of these, the prescription written on odd bits of paper which would pass from one person to another. Mother had a few of these. They included horrible-tasting liquorice powder for constipation, brimstone and treacle for the blood, quinine, hot rum and boiled onions for a feverish cold, and hot salt laid on your stomach in a stocking for all stomach pains. Pepper, vinegar and mustard on brown paper were advised for toothache. Sleeping tablets were absent from her list as were pills for nervous complaints. My father relied on a daily dose of beer and complained of no ailment until the end of his life at 65 years of age.

When people grew old and infirm and there were no children to care for them, the only place was the workhouse infirmary. Here married couples would be separated. We referred to such a sad ending as "going into the Lump" — an allusion to burial in a pauper's grave to save a few pounds on the rates.

Some people were untiring in their efforts to raise funds to help the hospitals with processions and carnivals through the streets, the most notable one being the Woodford Meet around Epping Forest. This consisted mainly of a procession of gaily coloured decorated vehicles — anything on wheels, in fact — often a mile long. It drew great crowds of people to empty their pockets.

There was one medical man practising in the East End of my youth who was very popular for a time until he let his side down. He was Doctor Jelley, a tall thin wiry man. He was an exhibitionist who went about the East End driving his own high dog cart. At first small boys began to call after him, parodying his name, but his very long cord whip soon silenced the boys. He only charged sixpence a visit and threepence for his physic if you provided your own bottle. He became popular, opened a couple of surgeries and a small maternity hospital in Homerton. Alas, he finished his versatile practice rather abruptly when he was found guilty in a case involving what was then, under the law, an illegal abortion.

The streets of the East End in those days were never free from morn to night of itinerant hawkers crying their wares. Many were physically handicapped, the like of which we do not see in our streets today. The morning started with cries of "Smoked 'addicks!", "Kippers!", "Bloaters!", "Milko!"; all competing, one or two selling skimmed milk at a penny a quart. During the day the street echoed the cries of "Dutch 'ens" (pickled herring), "Baker", "Oranges", "Greens" (vegetables), "Rock salt", "Baked taters", "Any ol' rags", "Cats meat", "Carbolic".

Each hawker had his or her own peculiar cry, many quite unintelligible from continual repetition. On Sundays the street cries took a different turn apart from the usual morning calls. We then had a few "down and outs", tramps, beggars singing hymns or playing a tin whistle. Then there would be the Salvation Army band rendering religious tunes, the lassies singing, marching in circles banging on their tambourines. On their way out of the street the lassies would call at every door with their blessing and a collection box. We had the benefit of the fellow crying out "five-a-penny comics" (back numbers), and beggars with or without tin whistles. About tea time we would have pedlars ringing hand bells, selling water "creases" (never "cresses"), muffins, "fine large shrimps", winkles, and "Suf'end (Southend) cockles".

"Sensational murder! Read all about it!" would be the favourite call of some newsboys late at night, passing through the streets disturbing everybody. The street then became alive, doors opened and a brisk trade done selling a piece of sensational news compressed into a few lines.

Revellers turned out of the public houses after midnight on Saturdays and were also a source of nuisance to neighbours and police alike. Our neighbour, Mrs May, had her own way of dealing with a group of night revellers who regularly disturbed her sleep on late Saturday nights. Perhaps it was the street lamp post outside her house that proved the magnet for a few revellers to tarry, drinking and singing after the street public house had closed at midnight. On the other hand it may have been her violent language and aggressive manner from her upstairs window that invited the serenaders continually to annoy her. She issued aspersions about their parentage and threatened what she would do to them if they didn't pack it up. She'd have called in the police but that would have been against the strict code, so she took the law into her own hands by emptying the contents of her chamber pot on their heads while they were singing. Mrs May was never troubled again but they sent her to Coventry for a long time afterwards.

Chapter 15

In my youth there were still the tot hunters, scratching around garbage bins and rubbish dumps, the workless searching the gutters for cigar and cigarette ends for breaking down and reselling. However, the collectors of "pure" (dog's dung) for the tanning trade had by then disappeared.

As late as the 1920s I saw street sellers in the New Cut, Lambeth, and in Brick Lane, Bethnal Green, with their two-wheel trolleys carrying copper pans containing boiling sugar. They were making cough drops and other medicinal sweets and would give away free samples to induce sales. There were also the gutter "chemists" selling tonics, rheumatic pills, corn cures, headache powders and the rest of the "cure all" offerings. On the Mile End waste there was a "dentist" selling tooth powder and extracting teeth free in order to attract an audience. There was only one thing that all these street traders had in common — the gift of the gab.

On occasions a "Dr Brown" would appear with a stethoscope around his neck (a sure winner for a sucker) dressed for the part in high hat and frock coat and address the crowd on the pains and ills that afflict mankind. If I listened to him long enough I felt that I needed his physic, which he would produce from his capacious bag. His son would be among the audience thrusting a bottle into one's hand for a shilling or two shillings for a large bottle. Next to him you would perhaps find a gutter "oculist" with his tray of lenses and spectacle frames prepared to test your eyes with a strip of newspaper held in front of you. Before he had taken this up he could have been any sort of a tradesman down on his luck from a dustbin maker to a tailor's presser. There was also the artist in modelling clay with easel and board creating a bust of William Shakespeare. When this failed he would be back trying to sell you a "wonder spy glass", which consisted of a tiny mirror glass set at an angle so that one could see people without them detecting that you were spying on them.

Street markets were never without a strong man lifting weights and bending crowbars and who probably had only had a slice of jam and bread for his breakfast that morning. Down and out actors entertained the crowd, and there were also the chalk pavement artist, the one-armed sailor darning pictures of boats with coloured wool. The Boer War "hero" selling matches in the gutter and displaying a pawn ticket to prove his medal "was up the spout".

On Saturday nights, the East End street markets were hives of activity, noise and bedlam. The stalls would be lit with naphtha flame lamps, the shops by naked gas jets. The noise was deafening with each stall holder and shopkeeper bellowing to the crowd as it pushed its way along the narrow pavement, and the itinerant hawkers cried about their wares. Little sneak thief urchins would slyly move about the stalls "lifting" anything edible within their grasp. It was not until midnight before the noise ceased and then the council workmen stepped in to clear away the debris.

I remember, too, the garret masters, who were makers of household furniture on their own account, selling their products to the dealers. My brother, William, left school in 1890 when he was 14, learnt a few tricks of the trade and set up on his own making mirror overmantels. He turned our bedroom into a daytime workshop, punched a hole through the ceiling and roof, without asking the landlord's permission, to take smoke from a portable fire stove on which stood the inevitable gluepot. The glue used in those days was not today's article, pressed out of tubes and smelling of lavender but the real, malodorous stuff.

After a time he must have saturated the market with his overmantels so he gave up the furniture line and started to learn electrical engineering, the first person in four generations of Southgates not to follow a dying trade.

Several of my school friends started work as garret masters. They either rented a room or bench room in any workshop about the East End. They specialised in leg tables, dining tables, nests of tables, sideboards, wardrobes or cupboards. Some were chair frame makers, providing frames for the upholsterer to finish, or they were french polishers, chairback carvers, table leg turners, or they inlaid the tops of tables or chests of drawers. What was turned out could be for the humble home or the mansions of the rich. The competition was intense and no outsider could equal these specialists for speed or price. As in Mayhew's day, they were largely at the mercy of the furniture firms who took much of what they produced on sale or return basis. Often they parted with their products at cheap prices just to keep alive. The influx into the trade during my youth of immigrants fleeing from their persecutors in Poland and Russia and settling in the East End added to their labour and housing problems.

This period coincided with the decline of that solid Victorian furniture which the old craftsmen turned out. In its place then began to develop cheap and shoddy treacle polish furniture of the sales firms openly advertising hire purchase terms. "Sent home in our plain-covered vans", an inducement to that great section of the community who frowned upon hire purchase as living beyond one's means. Nevertheless such people desired to keep up with the Joneses without loss of face and social status.

My father-in-law Wells was one of those Victorian craftsmen who was hit with the changing pattern of the times. In his early days he specialised in making six and eight feet solid walnut bay-fronted sideboards with wine cupboards under a spacious top, which required four men to move them into the dining halls of wealthy Victorian merchants. Afterwards my father-in-law switched over to high class upholstery work for the West End stores. He failed in this eventually and refused to come down to turning out shoddy stuff. He died as poor as he was born in a bed-sitter in one of these towering tenement blocks in the East End, alone with his one and only solid walnut sideboard which no junk merchant would take even as a gift because, as they said, there was no demand for that kind of thing.

However, his later years were not without light periods He found he was going bald prematurely and friends advised him to try all sorts of remedies to restore his disappearing hair. George R. Sims was at that time the versatile editor of *The Referee* and he advised Mr Wells to try his product called "Tacho". After Mr Wells had rubbed into his scalp the contents of two bottles and saw no visible evidence of even a single hair, in disgust he threw the third bottle on to a pile of broken chair frames lying at the bottom of his yard. Months later one of his daughters had occasion to visit the spot and come running back to tell her father that the chair frames were covered with what looked like hair!

We often used to speak of touching a person for money, often for a loan. This touching would often be practised by old lags just out of prison. Some, of course, were genuinely ex-prisoners but there were others who had made it a regular practice to accost pedestrians who looked likely to be "touchable". Old lags carried a printed card issued by a mission for discharged prisoners and flourished this in front of your eyes to prove their point. The card said: "Dear Friend, you are invited to partake of coffee, bread and butter, free of charge, at the Mission House, opposite the prison gates."

By the time I had left school I had heard, seen and experienced a little of the mendacity of the East End underworld around me but I had yet to experience the "respectable" imposter. On my various errands for father passing through the many streets and alleyways of the City of London I noticed a cripple, decently dressed, hobbling along in a most distressing manner and ostensibly selling matches. He was begging and begging was not allowed by the authorities unless you were selling something. I also noticed that he had made quite of collection of coins from passersby who never took his matches. However, one afternoon I was passing along the subway near the Bank of England when who should I recognise coming down the steps in a manner worthy of any schoolboy just freed from school but my cripple. He was racing to catch a train. I tipped off a policeman. The man was watched and subsequently convicted as a cheating rascal, who the authorities found was living in style in suburbia on the proceeds of ''selling'' matches.

Hoxton, in those days, was a notorious area where police at night walked in pairs. In some areas it was a hide-out for many skilled thieves and pickpockets. It was a habit of mine when I was working in Bishopsgate as an office boy to browse in my lunch breaks among the book barrows which stood at the kerbside outside the old Standard Theatre in Shoreditch High Street, One day, as I turned away after purchasing a secondhand book for twopence, I found myself minus my watch, a cheap 2s 11d Ingersoll.

Many weeks later I went to visit my Uncle Bill, who kept a small sweetshop and a couple of sweetstalls in the local Nile Street market and mentioned to him my loss. ''Why didn't you come to me at once'', he said. ''What could you have done?'', I asked. ''Done?'', he asked, ''I could have got that watch back in no time, of course. I know the fellows wot work that area and a pint of beer would have done the trick.'' He named the pub in Hoxton frequented by these pickpockets where they negotiated with the receivers.

It was said of Dr Christopher Addison when he represented Shoreditch in Parliament that at one of his meetings he had his pocket picked of his gold watch. Speaking of his loss immediately to one of his local supporters the latter promised that he would get it back for him and did so. The story goes that Dr Addison was presented later in his career with a gold watch on behalf of his supporters in recognition for services rendered to the constituency. Naturally he was much moved by their generosity knowing the appalling poverty of his supporters but the gift was a little tarnished as the police discovered the watch had been lifted from his Conservative opponent at one of the latter's meetings.

Chapter 16

Witnessing the building of huge stacks of timber on the banks of the Regent's Canal at the opposite side of our street was something that always interested me. The stacks would rise gradually in tall, square formation. They consisted of great baulks of timber unloaded from the barges by labourers, the timber coming to the Port of London from all parts of the world. No mechanical cranes were used in the unloading of barges or the stacking of timber. It was sheer hard manual labour. The labourers were almost bent double carrying the baulks of timber on their backs, walking up gang planks, erected zig-zag fashion on the outside of the pile as it progressed upwards. Tilers walking about the timber roof of a house with quantities of slates on their heads would be a comparable feat of skill and nerve.

Some stacks stayed in position for years so that they seasoned until they were sold. The roadways served also for fire breaks. To a child they were roads of sombre light eerie in their silence where ghosts, rats and goblins walked on moonlit nights. A watchman at night with his dog walked through these avenues to see that all was well and was ready to pounce on wanderers who dared to disturb the stillness of the night.

On the opposite bank of the canal there were other piles of timber but this was used for the packing box trade and consisted of different lengths of rough sawn stuff up to an inch in thickness. It was carried on men's backs in bundles and deposited on top of the huge stack for the stack builder to arrange. As these stacks began to build up internal staircases were formed. They served for ventilation as well as a means of easy access to the summit against the time dismantling began. We boys would race up and down these staircases which smelt of resinous pine. On top of such stacks we had a wonderful view of London's chimney pots of all shapes and sizes belching forth their smoke. Occasionally we would meet the big water rats which infested the place but they were only dangerous if you were foolhardy enough to try and corner them.

When the sawmills were busy and the mountain of timber began to diminish it was customary for boys of the area, intent on pocket money, to line up with sacks at the sawmill entrance gate. On the word from the foreman (after he had taken our pennies) we made a dash for the heap of offcuts and began eagerly to pack our sacks. Firewood was a useful and expensive fuel in our homes, especially on mother's washing days.

The canal towpath, along which horses pulled the barges, was out of bounds to the public: parents, police and canal authorities viewed the towpath as highly dangerous for children. Wire and wooden fencing, brick walls with a coping of iron spikes and broken glass set in cement were erected, yet we children managed to surmount these obstacles, as did those adults intent on suicide. We chose a particular spot where we had to climb a ten foot wall, making slots in the brickwork for hands and feet and then we would slide down an adjoining telegraph pole to the towpath below. We had an escape point some distance away, depending on from which end the policeman approached; the police never advanced simultaneously from both ends.

Ramps were placed along the canal to assist the barge horses should they stumble into the canal in a fog. The non-swimmers among us used these ramps for paddling. We ran about in the sun to dry ourselves. Only once do I remember our scouts giving a warning of police approaching. We gathered up our clothes and ran like fury as far as the ''Cat and Mutton'' Bridge or the old Gluemakers' Bridge at Old Ford before we paused to don a shirt and knickerbockers and then climb the iron railings to safety.

I can only once remember the canal being emptied for cleansing and the result was the revelation of its use as a rubbish tip. This can't have done us boys much good (though it apparently did not do us much harm either), but the absence in any of our homes of a bathroom was compensated for by the public baths, which I often used. There a towel, soap and as much hot water as we needed was provided by the council for 2d. (I remember many years later, when doing some gardening for James Hough, one-time headmaster of the Brentwood Grammar School, that he told me that when he was a young man at University College the question was raised of having proper bathrooms put in the university quarters. One old don remarked: ''Why go to all that expense and trouble? The fellows are only here for eight weeks a term''.)

Between the boys of North Street and the canal bargees there was perpetual feuding during the long summer holidays. This had gone on for many years, from one generation to the next. The boys had the advantage for we were on solid ground, fighting from the heights of Cambridge Heath canal bridge. The bargee had to steer under the bridge or put his barge in jeopardy in negotiating his passage. Precedent had established that bad language and missiles alone were used. As soon as the barge emerged from the tunnel at a signal from our captain a barrage of orange peel and rotten fruit would be discharged at the bargee. The bargee was prepared and his protests would be followed by a fusillade of mud clots. The campaign finished as it had begun, with no truce, and the boys had to return to school.

The boys, however, at the Whitmore Road, Hoxton, end of the canal had originated a more profitable plan for their part of the bridge. They never fought with the bargees for during the summer months they would be down on the footpath appealing to the bridge walkers to throw down their ''mouldy pennies'' into the water and they would retrieve them. They were artful. What the passerby on the bridge did not know was that beneath the murky water of the canal was stretched a long sheet of sacking so that not a coin was lost on the muddy bottom.

Children's haircutting in those days cost tuppence. The barber used hand-operated clippers, a smaller edition of those used for trimming horses. After we had our ''prison crop'', as it was called, we were allowed to go to a cupboard and select a small toy. This was usually a very cheap German-imported thing which, in those days, flooded the toy market.

Barbers' shops would have an array of china shaving pots each with a different number painted upon it and which stood on shelves around the shop. They were reserved for special customers. It was all in the interests of hygiene we were told as a precaution against ''barber's rash''. The odd thing about the precaution lay in the fact that nothing else in the barber's outfit was reserved to these ''special pots''. The cut-throat razor, used before the era of the safety razor, and everything else seemed to be used in common. The cut-throat razor of the barber was wiped on a piece of old newspaper or common towel, and cover sheets and hair brushes did for all. The floor was littered with the shorn locks of many clients, some of whose heads could not have been too clean.

Chapter 17

Having reached the elementary school leaving age of 14 in 1904, the problem arose of finding employment. Thrown into the vortex of a competitive labour market, where the boys of working class parents were considered ten a penny, this was no easy task, especially if one's father did not follow a skilled trade. My own father's trade was a rapidly dying one.

There were no employment exchanges or careers advice centres in those days. Left to my own devices I aspired to be an artist. My school boy ambition to become a fire engine driver had now diminished, and, unlike my elder brother, I had no liking for mechanical things. I found myself diligently reading newspaper advertisements seeking a job and walking round in circles looking for notices on factory gates and business premises displaying signs: "Boy required", "Sharp lad wanted", and so on.

With my headmaster's excellent character note extolling my worth and abilities as "industrious and willing, honest and recommended," my LCC Merit Certificate and my gold medal for not being late or absent once in seven years, I sallied forth with great hopes. Mother had smartened me up with a brand new starch collar, a bowler hat and a pair of long trousers ("to make a man of you", mother said because no East End boy of my time wore long trousers until he was 14 years of age). But, alas, there were thousands of other boys also smartly turned out by their mums and dads, also with character references as good as mine, all looking for elusive employment.

However, full of ambition, I had in mind that my drawings had some artistic merit and showed talent, I began to answer advertisements, one of which was by a firm engaged on church furnishing and mosaic work. Yes, my drawings impressed them but they wanted £20 as a premium for a seven year apprenticeship. During that time I would receive a few shillings a week as pocket money. To ask father to keep me until I was 21 was more than his flesh and blood would stand so that was scrubbed out.

My next effort was to answer an advertisement which stated: "Sculptor wants boy with talent. Apply with drawings, to Mr Sparrow, Oxford Street, W.1." I went along to see Mr. Sparrow, who turned out to be an understanding gentleman. I found him in his studio, dressed in a white overall among a collection of stone figures of angels and other statuary; he was holding a mallet and chisel. His fist remark on seeing my drawings was: ''Elementary stuff''. Nevertheless they showed promise, he said, when I explained that I had never had an art lesson in my life as I came from an elementary school. ''Just the ticket, my boy'', he said and my hopes rose. ''I don't want those art school kids coming here telling me how to do my job before they have lost the cradle marks off their backsides''. He asked me if I could help him to carve up Marble Arch. I said I could but I hadn't the slightest notion of where and what Marble Arch was or the magnitude of his question until father told me later that it was a leg pull. ''You're a bit short'', Mr Sparrow continued, ''but I'll find you a box to stand on to do the chipping''. I was ready for this. I said: ''I don't mind standing on a few boxes because, after all, sir Nelson was a small man wasn't he? And look where they had put him in Trafalgar Square''.

Then the blow fell. Mr Sparrow wanted a £20 premium, paying me pocket money for five years under an indenture. I said my father was a poor man and he offered to reduce the premium to £10 as he wanted to train an assistant in his own way to carve angels and statuary for the graves of rich clients.

When I told my father the terms, he at once put a cold blanket on the venture as he was not going to keep me at home on pocket money for five years, he said. There was now nothing for it but to take the first situation, pot luck, that offered itself. It might be as a messenger boy, a van boy, a shop boy or any other dead end job. The main consideration was that I had to bring a little cash into the home each week to feed myself.

It was in answer to another advertisement — ''Office boy wanted'' — that I queued with about 50 other boys in Bishopsgate Street, in the City. We lined up on the staircase, along the passage and out into the street. I surveyed my competitors. There were tall boys, short boys, fat boys and thin boys. All were like myself, turned out smartly by their mothers, full of hope and had come to this spot from the four quarters of London. Yet it seemed to me that I was the smallest of them all. The salary, which had attracted so many youths, was 6s a week.

None were turned away without an interview, a considerate proceeding and so different from the then prevailing callous custom of assembling a crowd of unemployed, many of whom had travelled long distances, only to be given short shift and briefly told: ''Suited''. The employer in this case was quite modest in his demands. He was not engaging a university don; just a boy to lick stamps, write addresses on envelopes and copy letters with the aid of a letter press. When it came to my turn to be interviewed, I walked into the gentleman's sanctum, a thickly carpeted room with a very large table in the centre covered with neatly arranged bundles of white and blue paper tied with pink tape. This was most awe-inspiring to me, heightened by the presence of many fat books and deed boxes, one on top of the other stacked against the walls. The silence was broken by a voice saying: "Write your name and address on this paper". The voice was that of Mr Roberts. He had placed before me a large used envelope cut open for the plain side to be written on, an economy I have copied ever since those days. He read my headmaster's character note, my merit certificate and said: "Very good". After all one could not be too careful when entrusting a strange boy in those days with 5s worth of postage stamps.

Why he should have chosen me amongst all that crowd of boys I cannot say but can only guess. With so many the choice may have depended upon the lucky dip from out of his high hat. Then again, it may have been my straight answers to his questions which may have intrigued him. Had I had any ambitions to become a solicitor? I answered firmly: "No". "Why not?', he asked, and I replied quite frankly: "I should never have the money, sir". I was thinking at the time that 6s would never get me very far up the legal ladder. I remember his saying: "That's a straight and sensible answer but if you ever get any money remember the profession is over-crowded".

The following Monday morning I was perched on a high stool at an equally high desk and receiving instructions as to the correct keeping of a postage book and the art of copying letters into a copying book with the aid of a screw press — a junior descendant it looked to me of one used by Caxton. The desk, as I soon found, was liberally chiselled with the initials of past generations of office boys with idle hands to employ. I wondered then where they had wandered to; whether any of them had become solicitors or judges or just nobodies; whether ghosts haunted those deed boxes and came out at night disturbing the accumulated dust of years and going back again at dawn with their pleadings unanswered and their appeals ignored.

On the ledge above my desk was a paraffin oil lamp for illumination during the winter months. In one corner of the room was a sink overlaid with lead sheeting, which was pockmarked with attempts at engraving by all previous office boys; accordingly I soon got going with my own penknife for the attention of posterity. Every inch of space in that room was occupied. Beside the old deed boxes packed with papers and documents of ancient and forgotten causes, there were stacks of dusty brown paper parcels, containing reports of all legal cases that had passed through the Courts of Justice since reporting began. There were dozens of letter books, numbered and indexed, which no one opened and if they had done they would be just as wise.

From the office window I could see the roof tops. The premises had been a private residence from the 17th century but was now past its best. Judging, however, by the picture I saw of it many years later in the nearby Bishopsgate Institute, donated by its owner, the artist wished to convey the impression that it had just emerged as a sweet little thing, so delicate and neat had he drawn his lines and applied his colours. Had that artist portrayed the interior of the premises in actual colour, the dark and twisted staircase which led to my employer's floor, it would have made a very different picture.

That staircase had much to answer for. My respect for the law was profound. The upholders of law and order and its professional advocates were indeed people who should not be trifled with. It was not surprising therefore, that judges, barristers and the like stood or sat on very high seats for me to worship. But one day, due to that dark and twisted staircase my adoration received a violent shock. Being a small person that staircase never troubled me, neither did it worry habitual users who instinctively ducked when they came to the bend. It caught the unwary, however, if they were in a hurry, as happened one day to a barrister of the tall skinny type, who came to see my employer. He was also a candidate for Parliament and was, therefore, in my eyes a very important person indeed. The time arrived and, with it, this exalted person. He mounted the first flight of stairs in a few bounds, but it was then I heard a crash and a stumble, followed by a torrent of bad language, the like of which I thought was only possible from the lips of our neighbour Mother Gurney when she was drunk. My dream of the advocates of the law as paragons of correct behaviour on all occasions was shattered — and so was this person's glossy top hat. I rushed out of the office door and down the staircase to salvage his head gear, while the candidate for Parliament sat down rubbing his head and muttering his curses about the staircase.

In the course of time, apart from keeping the postage book, addressing letters and running round the City and the Courts of Justice, I began to write up documents in "engrossing hand" and to "fair copy" barristers' briefs and opinions. A barrister's handwriting, like a doctor's, is atrocious. Although a great deal of what they wrote was incomprehensible to me I gradually learnt that their own special brand of shorthand consisting mainly of abbreviations: "indre" for indenture, "afsd" for aforesaid, "hrnfr" for hereinbefore, "intt" for interest, "ppal" for principal. It all seemed a strange and fantastic world to me, coming direct from the slums where pinching and scraping the bottom of the barrel were of paramount importance. In this office I was seeing people who came to talk, scheme and bargain in thousands of pounds about property and never about where the next loaf was coming from. Thus it was by reading their conveyances, leases, agreements, marriage settlements, wills, codicils and numerous other documents I got to learn, the stupendous amount of time, thought, energy and ingenuity that was expended by the Victorian middle class in making money, seeking it, hoarding it, investing it, settling it, speculating with it and spending it. Finally, if any was left when the time came to breathe their last, they tied it up for their progeny.

Such people were so cocksure as to the permanence of their institutions that if one had the temerity to challenge this concept they would immediately declare you were a subversive agent of a foreign power intent on breaking up their great British Empire. Nevertheless, they were taking no chances so they provided themselves against such a catastrophe in trust deeds and marriage settlements and so on. Clearly they were concerned not to leave their offspring high and dry without a shirt to their backs. They would be appalled at the idea that they should be reduced to invest in an alarm clock and turn out to work in the early hours of the morning in order to earn their own living.

"Lay not up for yourselves treasures upon earth where moth and rust doth corrupt." Such scriptural exhortations were taught to my generation of working class boys and girls as part of our school religious education; the eastern way of life where poverty was next to holiness was eulogised, not forgetting that a rich man had as much chance of entering the Kingdom of Heaven as he had of getting through the eye of a needle. Working in a lawyer's office, it was not long before it began to dawn upon me that there was a difference between preaching and practice. The work in that office, as in thousands of others throughout the great cities of the world, involved doing exactly the opposite to scriptural instructions. In my mind there was no sanctity about poverty, for few professing Christians believed it and certainly organised religion never practised it.

Chapter 18

It was part of my job as a junior clerk to walk the corridors of the High Court in the Strand and its labyrinth of spacious rooms and corridors as well as the courts themselves. This seemed of no account inside such a place. Every piece of business had to be stated on forms in duplicate and triplicate, which had to be lodged at the appropriate rooms. There was a heavy tome to study to get the right form in the right room and fees paid at the right room. Time was spent in leisurely going up and down staircases, over archways, under tunnels and through doors leading to more doors.

All business was conducted in a leisurely way between 10 am and 4 pm, but it was very wearing on the feet. So leisurely was the place that we clerks were even provided with quill pens to fill in the forms and the courts were among the last customers for the products of my father's skill. This would be about 1919 just after father died. Typewritten documents were discouraged some time after Queen Victoria died but, of course, eventually they were admitted and approved of.

Coaching me in the art of examining witnesses to ascertain the true facts, my employer pointed out that there was an old legal tag I should remember — the truthful, the lying and the expert witness. Serving writs and other legal documents on reluctant debtors had its adventures and pitfalls and took me into some queer places. I had to look for the customary dog, especially if it were off the chain as they usually were if the debtor was expecting proceedings. An owner of one such dog on whom I called assured me, while I kept at a comfortable distance: "He's a friendly dog really: you should know the old proverb, 'A barking dog never bites'". "Yes", I replied, "we both know that but does that dog know the proverb, too?" I took no chances with such a "friendly dog" so I got a substituted order against the owner on the ground that while the owner was friendly, his dog was ferocious. I had passed the job to the postal service.

I had the curious experience once of serving a writ on a "corpse". It was at the time I was very green at the work but I had to make a start and this particular writ was for an undertaker in Wapping, East London. He was an elusive customer and could have easily been served while conducting a funeral but that did not strike me as the right thing to do, so I went to his shop and hoped for the best. I looked through his front shop window set out in the usual mournful style of the period and saw there was a door at the far end of the shop. I slipped through the shop, opened this door and found myself in a workshop full of wood shavings and half-finished coffins. There were no workmen about but my sudden appearance had been seen by a man at the far end who had immediately stepped behind a few coffins set upright on the floor. Wishing to disguise the fact that I had seen him, I called out several times: ''Mr Noakes''. There was no answer so I slowly walked to the spot where I had seen him disappear: there was no Mr Noakes. I walked behind the few coffins standing on their ends and began to get keyed up when suddenly I noticed one of the coffins had a velvet horsecloth loosely drawn over it. This I tore away and there facing me standing upright was my ''corpse'', Mr. Noakes. I never stopped to make enquiries, promptly thrust the writ between his legs and rushed out of the shop as fast as my legs could carry me.

I had a summons once to serve on an old man who lived in a mean little street near St George's Circus, Southwark. It was a rack-rented tenement house like all the rest in the street. The whole place shouted poverty. The front door of the particular house I wanted was wide open for anyone. There was no carpet covering the passage way or the staircase; just bare wood and that caked with dirt. The balustrade on the staircase had disappeared, for firewood, no doubt. I stood in the passageway wondering whether my business was worth bothering about when an old woman, partially clothed and not too clean, came out of a side door. She said: ''Wot d'yer want?''. ''Does Mr Mears live here?''. ''Yus, fust floor, door on left''. Then she added: '''E's ill. 'Ave yer got 'is rent?''. ''No'', I replied and proceeded up the well-worn staircase. I knocked on the door and heard a faint reply: ''Come in''.

The sight that met my gaze appalled me. I had been used to scenes of poverty all my life but this was rank squalor. The stench from that room was overpowering. The man I wanted was lying on a wooden couch covered with sacking and an old army great coat. The hearth and fireplace were choked with spent ashes and kitchen garbage. In the corner was a pail of urine and ordure filled to the brim. As I looked down at the man I said: ''How long have you been laying like this?'' ''Over a week'', he replied, ''my leg's bad,'' and he lifted the sacking and showed me a filthy, ulcerated limb which smelled to the ceiling. ''Have you a doctor?'', I asked. ''No, what's the good, they'll only order me away to the work 'ouse''. ''Surely it will be better than all this?'' I replied. ''I'd be 'orrit soon if it wasn't for this 'ere blasted leg. That 'ol cow downstairs wants me out 'cause I ain't got the rent. I can manage a bit o' grub''.

Looking down on this derelict specimen of humanity it struck me forcibly why was it that such people hang tenaciously on to what they know and why they have a holy horror of going into the lump or the workhouse which to them was really the end. In his case he was fighting a battle which was already lost. I came away from that stinking hovel sick in my stomach. I gave the old woman a few shillings to buy the old man some food and clean the place up. I rang the medical officer of health to tell him of the man's condition. He had him removed to the infirmary but it was too late. He was dead in a week. I forgot my summons. He had a higher one.

It was then customary practice amongst solicitors to have their correspondence and documents written by hand and clerks were engaged for their calligraphy and beautiful work, especially when it came to engrossing on parchment. I saw perhaps the last of the old-time scriveners or writers. By the nature of their work they sometimes worked all through the night either fair copying or engrossing deeds for which they were paid by the folio (72, 80 or 90 words). The few old men I knew were snuff takers and always had a can of beer at their elbow while they worked.

Old Clematis was one such old timer, employed in Tooley Street by London Bridge. His employers finally objected to Old Clematis bringing cans of beer into the offices as they thought it lowered the tone of the place should clients see them. But the old boy was not put off or dismayed for he had found a way round their edict. Visiting the pub meant losing time as he was employed on the folio basis, so with the aid of a pub crony he managed to get his supply of beer under his desk and his employers were none the wiser.

The office building was one which had a set of windows facing Tooley Street serving rooms occupied by partners of the firm and another set of windows facing the back street with rooms assigned to the staff. It was just a matter of routine about refreshment times for Old Clematis, on hearing the familiar whistle of his boozy pal in the back street, to open the second storey window and let down his empty beer can on a hook and line. This crony would then take off the empty can and hook on a full can of beer which Old Clematis hauled up. So this cycle of beer haulings would go on intermittently all day to the wonderment and curiosity of the employers, who towards the evening, naturally saw evident signs in their scrivener's gait which wasn't all it should be for a sober man. When we juniors heard the whistle we used to say to one another: "Haul away! Hook, line and sinker!"

It was a great day for me when I had my first ride in a two-wheel hansom cab. It was ordered to take my employer and myself to the Law Courts. We packed the cab with a whole lot of books, all carefully earmarked with slips of paper, and climbed in among them. Off we went, I feeling quite regal by the side of Mr Roberts. We travelled down Bishopsgate Without, past St Botolph's Church when we entered Bishopsgate Within*. We passed the Bank of England, which had an ugly stone wall around it at that time, and then went on to the Law Courts via Ludgate Hill. Arriving at the courts I deposited the books in one of them.

Walking about were many learned counsel in their wigs and gowns, many of which looked frayed and the worse for wear.

During the lunch break Mr Roberts gave me sixpence to get myself a sandwich which I consumed standing in a cold meat snack bar in Chancery Lane.

None of the books and volumes of correspondence which we had brought were referred to in court. They were not wanted to prove or disprove anything. I mentioned this fact to Mr Roberts as we journeyed back to the office in the horse cab and he looked down at me and said: "It is a principle of our law system, Southgate, that justice must not only be done but that nothing should be left to chance to stop it being done."

---

*These terms, now no longer used, refer to the time when London (or what is now called the City of London) had been surrounded by a wall. One of the entries was at Bishop's Gate, thus "Without" and "Within" designated on which side of the wall the road ran.

Chapter 19

As a boy of the streets, I had never been averse to earning pocket money by accosting people and offering to carry their parcels. In cases where I was given my fare I never thought of using it. I walked, occasionally getting rides on the back of horse carts or tram cars which happened to be going in my direction.

I persisted in this same habit crossing the City of London. The horse bus fare from Bishopsgate to the Strand was 2d or the "Tup'ney Tube" to any number of stations. During my lunch break of one hour I would spend my time eating sandwiches walking around Liverpool Street Station observing trains coming and going. Watching other people at work had an attraction for me as it has for most people with time on their hands and little money in their pockets. It was certainly interesting for me to watch three or four sturdy labourers in the streets, before the introduction of the pneumatic drill, swinging their 14lb hammers in rhythmic unison driving a steel drill into thick concrete before it would crack, or I would watch the railway porters descend in clouds on to a platform waiting for the incoming long distance trains with a practised eye on their "tips" which they needed to supplement their 14s a week wages. Also hovering around the station were pirate or outside porters, each working on their own account ready to pounce on a likely passenger, and between the two kinds of porters there was a constant feud. Many were the tricks and devices these pirates practised to dodge the railway police and official porters in order to sidle up to a passenger and offer to carry their parcel or direct them to the right bus, if needed. For the pirates it must have been a precarious living, measured in coppers, as they were obviously, from their apparel, waifs and strays living rough and sleeping either in doss houses or on the embankment in sheets of newspaper. However, at that time, a shilling would keep a man from sheer starvation for at least three days.

While working as an office boy in Bishopsgate, I still had ambitions to become an artist but where and how to train for such a calling and make it a bread and butter proposition was far beyond my comprehension. Doubtless, I was a starry-eyed youngster who puzzled and scared a father on whom one could not depend as a guide and counsellor because it was beyond his ken. The best I could do in such circumstances was to attend an evening school to get the necessary training. I, therefore, enrolled as a pupil at the Sir John Cass's Institute, South Hackney, taking for my subjects, art and commercial and municipal law.

I was soon left wondering what the LCC paid the art master for;

certainly not to teach me or any other beginner. I saw him for less than three minutes on the few evenings I attended. He gave me no outline or scheme of work to follow, and no books that I could consult when I explained my purpose. It was painfully obvious to him that I was an "elementary" with an idea of making a bread and butter living from his beloved art. He danced attendance on a group of young ladies behind their easels, who, for all I could see, were learning art for art's sake at the public expense. To this cultural effort I could see no objection. It was no doubt a very pleasant occupation for the drawing room providing that the same ratepayer's money was also spent on helping "commercials" to gather knowledge. My effort having thus misfired after a few evenings paddling my own canoe, I gave it up and from that day ceased to bother about "art" until many years later, with greater leisure on my hands, I renewed my interest in calligraphy as a hobby.

I did much better with my legal studies, yet I had to admit that I had no aspirations for staying in the law to earn my living, but I had no desire to vegetate in an office as a mere pen pusher. I was fortunate in having for my teacher, Mr Guthrie, a Hackney solicitor who was a different character from the snobbish art master. Mr Guthrie said my papers showed promise and was prepared to go to some lengths to help me to pass the preliminary examinations. This was one golden opportunity that did come my way but I declined it, conscious at the time no doubt that my social background would never get me far in a profession which I already knew was overcrowded and badly paid so far as the pen pushers were concerned. It was as much as I could do, like the youthful Kipps, to keep "respectable", dressed in a secondhand suit and a much-brushed bowler hat.

I continued my evening school studies for a number of years after I was 14. I was what one would call a late developer, winning many prizes for various subjects, including a principal prize in an essay competition for the whole of London evening schools. This book prize was presented to me by the Prince of Wales, afterwards to become King George V, a rare distinction for an East End elementary school boy of those days and one of which I am modestly proud.

I never held it against my parents that they could have done better for themselves and their children had they asserted themselves and moved away from the stultifying effects of East End life to the suburbs then growing in Ilford, Edmonton and Walthamstow. They were part of the East End and were no better or worse than any of its other inhabitants.

The community spirit would be gone in any new effort to live aloof behind the suburban garden hedges, boarded fences and locked doors. My parents would have felt like fish out of water; the quietness, privacy and lack of neighbourliness would have overwhelmed them and made them miserable. Gone would be the friendly chats at the street door on a summer evening, the mutual help when in need, the bustling street market stalls and the atmosphere of the public house. And as for keeping up with the Joneses, one of the characteristics of suburban life, my parents didn't care a fig.

Thus, despite everything, I remained a member of the order into which I was born.

Chapter 20

My father's political views as a radical of the Charles Bradlaugh school influenced me greatly in taking an interest in social and political economy. He believed in Henry George's land reform and nationalisation, Home Rule for Ireland, no religion in schools, and, unlike most men of his time, he supported women's suffrage. Considering that in his time only about half the adult male population had votes I do not think he took the subject very seriously, often making jokes as men did of what women would do when faced with certain situations, and finally ending with the remark: "Well, they can't make a worse mess of things than men have done."

In his own youth, following the practice of his radical father, he took an active interest in politics and did his share in attending demonstrations and gatherings (though my mother always said: "It's a chance for him to meet his pals for rounds of drinks and blow the froth").

As a youth he had, with his father, got mixed up in the Hyde Park railings affairs. An attempt was made to close the park and met with radical resistance and when father climbed a tree to dodge police batons, he had fallen and injured his arm. He well remembered, also, "Bloody Sunday" in November 1887, in Trafalgar Square, when the police and the army dispersed a political demonstration, and many other turbulent meetings.

Father claimed that on "Bloody Sunday" the Government and the leisured classes of the West End had got the jitters when they saw crowds of marchers, many in their tattered clothes and looking toil-worn, marching past their mansions and clubs, led by such fire-eating orators as John Burns, Tom Mann, H.H. Campion and the top-hatted Marxist H.M. Hyndman. Then there was the sight of Cunninghame-Grahame leading on a white horse and Campion issuing orders like some military officer deploying contingents of troops to frustrate the efforts of the police at suppression and diversion. Father was very proud of his part in these affairs and described Government measures as "corkstoppers to plug the ship's boiler".

Later in life he became an armchair politician and pontificated most eloquently from his corner of the kitchen with a pint of "'arf and 'arf" (light and bitter) at his elbow. He fulminated against the sins of the Tory Government, the wealth and hypocrisy of all organised religion and the inequality of opportunities in the vicious social system that they upheld. "No wonder," he said, "We are people without religion."

Mother had no time for his "polishticks", as she called it, and would often interrupt with: "For Gawd's sake, Bill, give it a rest". Then he would look ruefully into his jug of beer and add: "I fort so, the 'ead's orf it. It's as flat as Muvver McGinty's feet."

As a boy I would sit in that small kitchen, using the free end of the table absorbed in my homework. However, at times, I could not escape my father's arguments as I was the only one in the house to either question or contradict his comments as he read out loud from his newspaper, usually the *Reynolds' News,* which was his bible.

He was a supporter of Gladstone and, finally, Lloyd George. Father never lived long enough, however, to see his Welsh radical hero kill the Liberal Party as an effective force, making a deal with the wealthy and the privileged for whom father had the greatest contempt.

On his death I found that father had been a founder-member of the Dove Row, Haggerston, Radical Club, where he had paid many a penny in the "penny-a-brick" scheme to help build it. In those days the scheme worked by "selling" bricks for a penny or sixpence; small cards were printed as a recognition of the "sale". Father had done his bit there, too.

Chapter 21

No society is unchanging and when I became interested in the harshness of the ''living in'' system which was the lot of the shop worker before the First World War, I joined in the movement to get it changed. In 1905 I became a member of the Social Democratic Federation*.

I recall that the shop assistants organised a great meeting, securing Bernard Shaw and the Countess of Warwick to speak on their behalf. Such were the fears of victimisation by some employers that it was arranged that when shop assistants acted as sandwichboard men advertising the meeting throughout the City and the West End of London, they would wear masks for fear of being identified. I joined in this masked parade although I was not in the shop trade but I believed in their cause.

I was undoubtedly an angry young man of my time, impatient with those in Parliament, who were only touching and fiddling with the fringe of problems, while there was a cauldron of misery, poverty and unemployment boiling under their noses. The Liberal Government of Sir Henry Campbell-Bannerman, which could have done a great deal with its huge majority, frittered away its energies and powers on trifling matters. It was at this time that I deserted father and his radicalism, feeling convinced that the Liberal Party in power was in the pockets of big business interests and its radical wing a dying force.

On most Sunday mornings I attended Speakers' Forum near the band stand in Victoria Park. Here I thirsted for information on all sorts of subjects. Speaking there were flat earth theorists, bimetallists, secularists, revealed religion advocates, Christian Evidence enthusiasts, anarchists and socialists, as well as all the other cranks and clowns with the gift of the gab who were sure of an audience which enjoyed itself immensely by heckling without coming to blows. The lesson this taught me was to try to sift a few grains of wisdom from the sack of chaff offered by each budding Demosthenes. This was the free speech which we all took for granted and which I realised was one of this country's greatest assets in being a safety valve.

---

*The Social Democratic Federation had been founded in 1881 as the Democratic Federation (the change of name took place in 1883) by an ex-conservative journalist and stockbroker H.M. Hyndman, a Marxist. It was the first modern socialist body, and for a short time it numbered William Morris as a member.

In those days there were three main socialist bodies, the Independent Labour Party*, the Fabian Society** and the Social Democratic Federation. There were also offshoots, splinter groups wrangling about the best way to achieve the end product but getting nowhere.

The Fabians seemed very remote, giving me the vision of middle class intellectuals like Bernard Shaw and the Webbs, with numerous blueprints of an ordered society run by a master race of scientific technicians. To me, however, the greatest obstacle was to break through the mass of apathy and ignorance among my own working class. They had first to be organised and educated in socialist economics and to learn to be critical and wary of ambitious politicians.

The Independent Labour Party as a propagandist body was full of idealism, attracting many "change of heart" advocates, stressing a strong ethical flavour, and intent on capturing the electoral machine as an instrument of power. It was weak on economics and good on reforming society.

As I became more and more involved in my political interests, joining this body and going to that meeting, one of the characters I met very early on and whom I revered up to the time of his death was George Lansbury, who was later to become leader of the Labour Party. His pioneering work on behalf of the poor and the downtrodden, especially in his beloved borough of Poplar, was inspiring. My future mother-in-law was his wife's sister, so later I was to have a family connection with him.*** I looked upon him as a great man with a heart of gold.

There remained the Social Democratic Federation which I joined having been attracted to it by the forthright meetings and speeches of H.M. Hyndman and Harry Quelch, the latter being expelled from Stuttgart for calling the Allied Commission a "thieves' kitchen". He was also editor of the party's journal, *Justice.* The very mention of the party's name struck terror in the minds of the leisured classes, who saw

---

*The ILP was formed in 1893 with the object of co-ordinating the efforts of trade unions to gain parliamentary representation without Liberal support. It helped form the Labour Representation Committee in 1900 which in 1906 became the Labour Party. The ILP continues its existence but has not won a parliamentary seat since 1959.

**The Society is a non-Marxist propagandist body founded in 1893-4 which has been at times very influencial within the Labour Party.

***But he had more extensive family ties with the Left in that one of Lansbury's daughters married Ernest Thurtle, former mayor of Shoreditch and MP for that constituency, while another married Raymond Postgate, the socialist historian and Lansbury's biographer, who was himself the brother of Margaret Cole, another socialist historian, and she had married G D H Cole, economist and Fabian Society theoretician.

violent anarchy stalking the land which, of course, was a lot of baloney. H.M. Hyndman, resplendent in top hat and black frock coat, was the quintessence of a rich Victorian gentleman. He was about the most supreme optimist I ever met. To him the revolution was just around the corner. The venerable old gentleman died peacefully in his bed at a ripe old age, breathing fire and hate against the Germans and to hell with his hitherto socialist principles.

In 1916 I was one of three objectors to conscription for what we thought was a capitalist war for markets who called on him at his home in Queen Anne's Gate, Westminster, to have him explain to us his bellicose attitude in actively supporting the war. He met us in a friendly manner and explained his attitude and we came away realising that he was still a capitalist at heart with a hatred of German policy to invade English markets and spheres of influence and that he was prepared to fight to keep them out. With this bellicose attitude there could be no peace in the world.

I recall an earlier meeting with Hyndman when he was a speaker at a meeting in my native Hackney in 1907. It was to welcome Victor Grayson upon his election to Parliament for the Colne Valley Division, a victory which, at the time, was a landmark. I was a young 17 year old steward at that meeting and took the opportunity to have a few words with him. Victor was certainly an evangelist and an inspiration to all young people with his brilliant flow of language fired with enthusiasm. Unfortunately, in later years, he showed instability of character and became an alcoholic.

One day he walked out of his home, having lost his seat as MP, and disappeared without trace. His body was never found. My theory about his disappearance is as good as the next. In a drunken state he may have wandered and fallen into the pestiferous chemical waste and mud of the River Lea marshes. The place was well known as a death trap and had been misgoverned by seven local authorities each with rights there. Within a short time a body once trapped would rot without trace.

The 1907 meeting was chaired by Robert Blatchford, a very rare thing for him to do. He figured very much in my early life. He was a leading protagonist for the socialist cause. He had been a soldier before the turn of the century and had founded *The Clarion* newspaper in 1891. He was no speaker but a power with his pen. His book *Merrie England* had a phenomenal sale of over a million copies.

On the outbreak of the 1914-18 War he became a warmonger like so many other socialists and from that time his newspaper declined in circulation and finally folded. With it declined the various activities of the numerous Clarion groups. In 1913 I was editor and compiler of the *Clarion Year Book* for 1914, a 48-page volume giving a complete account of the numerous Clarion societies, groups, interests and activities: the war killed all further publications.

Soon after I joined the Social Democratic Federation the comrades made me secretary of the South Hackney Branch. As holder, too, of the purse strings of all 20 of us, I had to make my quarterly report. "Comrades — income from subscriptions and collections is £6 2s 4d; rent of room, postage, leaflets £6 1s. Cash Balance 1s 4d," I said, adding: "Our respected leader Hyndman reminds us that the revolution is just round the corner. May I remind you that we have over 8,000 voters in this constituency and we have 1s 4d to take us round that corner." I was quite serious but all my pals laughed and I did, too, when I had time to size up the problem of running a revolution on 1s 4d in an area as big as South Hackney.

Not long after this, in 1905-6, I and six others founded the Hackney branch of the National Union of Clerks and I became its chairman. I also acted as a delegate to the Hackney Trades Council. I was also the NUC representative to the Labour Representation Committee. The LRC had been founded in 1900 and its secretary was an Independent Labour Party delegate, James Ramsay MacDonald. The Labour Party, as such, did not come into being until 1906 and it was not until 1918 that individual membership of the party was possible. As I write, only myself and Lord Shinwell survive as original members of the LRC.

It was while I was chairman of the NUC branch that in 1919 then plain Mr Herbert Morrison (later Lord Morrison of Lambeth) came along to join the union. He was to become mayor of Hackney in 1920-1 and MP for South Hackney, but in the early years we were neighbours in Upper Clapton. I remember that he was running around London trying to form local Labour parties on a sausage-and-mash salary, and I was running about on my spare evenings talking to groups and trades councils to try to organise white collar workers who were either too snobbish to associate with grimy gasworkers or who were frightened of their employers.

Herbert, I came to think, had a bee in his bonnet about Communists. Perhaps he had cause to as they seem to have conducted a vendetta against him as a result, I assume, of some cloak and dagger directive of the party's inner circle. Herbert even thought I was a Communist or at least a fellow traveller, though I was not and never have been. Some communists who had joined the branch had found that Herbert's dues were in arrears, and they made public this as evidence of his betraying the working class. One night after a meeting I mentioned the arrears to Herbert. I meant no criticism and only wanted to get the matter settled as quietly as possible. All Herbert did was to snap back bitterly: "Have you, too, joined the Communists? I'll send you a cheque". He did, indeed, pay up but forever afterward he treated me coldly.

Like so many other Labour leaders he was all for the huge and efficient voting machine dangling the necessary carrots to get the voters to the poll. I was more interested in educating people in socialist economics and policy and not in the least interested in harnessing "rebels" to vote as the be-all and end-all of socialist activity. And so with a few other members of the Social Democratic Federation I would hold street corner meetings. It was often my job to take the chair by standing on a wooden soap or sugar box. We would do this (and in comparative safety for this was before the age of the motorcar) until we were moved on by a policeman. Then we would be off to look for another street corner.

But to return for a moment to the Communists in the time between the wars (the heyday of their organisation). My view was that they were a group of young and politically motivated, immature rebels who fell into the error of believing that history began the day they took out membership and went to bed with Joe Stalin.

One I came to know through unusual circumstances was William Rust, one time (and the best known) editor of the *Daily Worker* (now the *Morning Star*) and a respected member of the party.

He was 18 years old when I first knew him and he was employed as a junior clerk at the Hulton Press; he was also a member of my union, the National Union of Clerks. He borrowed "copy" and a cheque from Sir Edward Hulton's office desk. He turned this over to Jack Tanner, then editor of the Left wing paper, *Solidarity* (and afterwards an official of the Amalgamated Engineering Union) for photographing and returning to Sir Edward's desk within the hour without being spotted.

The object of all this was to expose J.T. Brownlie, the then president of the engineering union, who was writing for the Hulton Press under the guise of "our Labour correspondent". This was considered highly suspicious in the eyes of a good many Communists. Scotland Yard lost no time in discovering the borrower and Sir Edward Hulton sacked his junior clerk and refused to prosecute. When Sir Edward asked Rust if he had no sense of loyalty towards his employer, Rust replied: "Where the workers' interests are concerned I owe no allegiance or loyalty to any employer — good or bad."

Rust told me all this when he came to me begging for a job after many months of unemployment as the bar was against him in the printing trade. I engaged him on my temporary staff to break the discrimination that other employers showed against him. I did not expect any medals for what I did for him, but I did not expect, however, rudeness when his employment ended and ungracious remarks upon parting about my being a "bosses' man". He had known full well that the job was a temporary one.

Chapter 22

The decade before the outbreak of the 1914-1918 war showed signs of unrest and a quickening interest among the working classes, and particularly so among those of my generation. The intense propaganda activity of the various socialist parties was having its effects on mass apathy. The flood tide of street corner oratory was at its height and loudest. For example, in the issue of *Justice* for 10 July 1909 there were 120 meetings advertised for that week in London alone. If we add to that number meetings by the Independent Labour party, the Clarion Scouts and all the other splinter groups the number must have been immense. The sales and free distribution of literature were remarkable.

During this same period unemployment was rife throughout the country, although no official figures were kept. Labour exchanges had still to come into existence. The figures could only be guessed at and gauged by statistics kept by a few trade unions for skilled workers which showed that 9.5 per cent of their membership was out of work. This was high compared with the economists' two per cent "safe margin" in a capitalist economy. Therefore, the figure of mass unemployment for unskilled labourers must have been very high indeed.

The utter indifference and callousness of Parliament to tackle seriously a social canker because the victims were largely an inarticulate and unorganised mass provided the socialist with abundant amunition to exploit the prevailing discontent. This was building up to a crescendo when the 1914 war came along and the idle workless found themselves either laying down their lives as soldiers fighting for King and Country or busy at work on the war effort.

In a local effort at Hackney during this pre-war period, I remember the local socialists decided that only shock tactics would frighten the smug, middle-class voters out of their skins. It was an easy salve to their consciences by constantly saying that the unemployed were work shy; therefore, shocks would get some at least to appreciate the dangers and explosive nature of social discontent. George Oram, a veteran of the Boer War, was to lead a poster parade through the wealthier parts of Hackney and I was deputed to prepare the posters, the markings on which would be skull and cross bones, skeletons, starving children and other macabre stuff. There were 12 of us, with George at the head wearing his medals and carrying a large red flag, the latter calculated to send shivers down the spines of comfortable drawing room viewers. Each sandwichman carried a poster fore and aft and wore a mask for fear of victimisation. At the rear of our procession a comrade blew a blast on his bugle at intervals. In the meanwhile any unemployed fellows were ostentatiously busy ringing at door bells and pushing handbills into letter boxes explaining that unemployment was a social responsibility and could not be salved or solved by charity and soup kitchens but by government action. We carried no collection boxes as a sign of our sincerity. As a publicity stunt, with a moral and educational purpose, this was something new and it brought us many recruits from this quarter of the borough.

On another occasion the proposed visit of the Czar of Russia in 1909 to this country called forth much public indignation. Whitehall got really alarmed about the nationwide protests. They compromised by allowing King Edward VII to meet the Czar at sea. The Home Secretary got the wind up and confiscated an issue of *Justice* which carried a cartoon, "The Czar's Nightmare", depicting Czar Nicholas jumping aside in horror from an exploding bomb. Hackney socialists promptly organised a poster parade through the borough to exploit the situation and strengthen the opposition to his visit to England. I was asked to make several enlarged drawings of the cartoon. We had a most successful parade and the police did not confiscate those posters.

In 1908 the Social Democratic Federation put up a candidate for the parliamentary constituency of Haggerston, which was both my mother's birthplace and that of Charles Bradlaugh. It was predominantly a working class area where poverty, squalor and pockets of petty crime flourished. The Federation's candidate was without the funds and election machinery that Liberals and Tories possessed but the few members had a colossal amount of faith, cheek and enthusiasm. The conspiracy of silence by the entire press and the two major parties, the ignorance of the masses of what socialism was and was not as well as their hostility had to be broken down. Hence the election was more of a publicity and advertising campaign for socialism than anything else. It was votes that achieved power. Taking the average national figures of the times as applying to this constituency only about half of the adult population of Haggerston had the right to vote.

The advent of an avowed socialist in Herbert Burrows, a retired civil servant, was one of the early landmarks in electioneering as a means of propagandising and brought a touch of reality to the problems affecting the lives of common working people. His programme was a lengthy document covering four pages, but in those days people liked it that way. He stood for complete adult suffrage (at that time not all men had the right to vote); payment of members in national and local government, and the payment of election expenses from national funds; and proportional representation. He also believed in the abolition of the

House of Lords, the disestablishment of the Church of England; and free, compulsory secular and technical education. Mr Burrows called for dwellings to be built and let at economic rents; and the nationalisation of land, thus preparing the way for full employment of our national resources. He wanted the taxation of land values, believing that the poor are poor because they have been robbed by the rich, and extensive death duties; and graduated income tax. His programme also included an eight hour day, improvement of the Factories and Workshop Acts, wage boards and a minimum wage to deal with the worst cases of sweated labour; abolition of the Poor Law, and the substitution of old age pensions, along with free dispensaries and municipally run hospitals. On the question of the liquor traffic, local option was needed but the real solution — the improvement of people's homes and municipal restaurants — was required. There should be, said Mr Burrows, international peace by arbitration, Free Trade and tariff reform and Home Rule for Ireland, while India would be given self-government. Civil service posts should be opened to all, he declared.

Mr Burrows stated in his address: "I declare my faith as a socialist in the ownership and control of the means of production and material necessities of life and by voting for me you will help to pave the way for a higher mental and nobler moral life for the individual and the nation at large."

When that programme was first launched upon the proletariat of Haggerston the socialists were called "visionaries" and it was said not to be practical. Yet I have lived to see many of the proposals accomplished but I'm also mindful of the fact that Rome wasn't built in a day.

We once had a voter who expressed himself on the ballot paper as a dissatisfied customer. It was the local Clapton ward election many years before the First World War. The ballot paper contained no less than 36 candidates for nine seats. So long was the ballot paper that when opened in the polling booth cubicle it hung down like a roll of wallpaper. This presented the voter with quite a problem if he was intent on voting for his party's ticket. In large letters this one voter wrote across the ballot paper: "Bugger the lot of you".

There was a great deal of covering up and defacing one another's election posters in those days. One poster reading: "Vote for good old Alf", a wag had altered to read: "Vote for good old Ale". There was one occasion when a brewery firm used the slogan: "Our beer is best", and the Temperance supporter had added words so it read: "Our beer is best left alone."

In the South Hackney election of 1905 I recall a poster: "Vote for Robertson, your old and tried member." Horatio Bottomley's agent issued a rejoinder: "Vote for Robertson — your old and tired member". It was generally known in political circles that Mr Robertson, the

Conservative member, had made only one speech in his five years at Westminster. Bottomley's agent went one better and printed a handbill: "Mr Robertson has only opened his mouth once and that was when he got up and asked the Speaker: 'Sir, could we have the window shut?' ".

My first experience of electioneering had been when I was ten years old. It was during the "Khaki Election" of 1900. Not that I knew anything about politics but children were used by the parties as part of their campaigning and, bribed with sweets, they distributed handbills.

Chapter 23

From 1905 onwards I saw the great Horatio Bottomley at most of his meetings and a great deal of hullabaloo went on with his electioneering. There was a great deal of personal bitterness by some candidates (most of it feigned) and shadow boxing on issues like whether wet fish should be sold on Sundays but there was no one dealing with the real economic problems and the mass poverty.

I knew — and it was confirmed in later years when the whole story came out — that Horatio's camp followers influenced voters in South Hackney in ways that would never be tolerated today. No money was spared in this subtle game of near bribery. There were public house outings for mothers and children to the country, Christmas gifts and mysterious "free nights" on the public house when his camp followers, Perkins, Houston, Cox and others, turned up in the saloon bar for a drink. Public house news travelled fast and drinks were on them. No sports club was refused a subscription provided Horatio's name appeared as a donor. He was adept at beating the big drum of patriotism which fed on war hysteria of the times. He was the biggest confidence man among gamblers, a tribe who indulged in big talk, big deals, speculation and bogus company promoting to further their ends. He never questioned his conscience about using other people's cash in his money-spinning schemes or asking their permission. He knew the legal technique for silencing critics, knowledge gained as an experienced official court shorthand writer. His worship of money and extravagance in spending it threw up some curious sides to his character. He was caught travelling on the railway from his home in Sussex to London and back, bilking his fare for quite a long time. When he came to South Hackney to nurse the constituency, he was in a way on home ground, brought up as he was by the Holyoake family who lived in St Peter Street, off the Hackney Road. Not all the Liberal people were taken in by him, and certainly not the few local socialists and trade unionists, either by his persuasive promises of rewards, threats of legal proceedings or claims to his political honesty.

It was known in political circles in South Hackney in the late 1890s that Horatio Bottomley was making overtures to the local Liberal Party executive, coupled by his presence at all the local clubs and the like, to get himself adopted as their parliamentary candidate. Without a shadow of doubt, he had laid his plans to get into Parliament to further his money-making ambitions and, like a good many more, to mix in the right circles where money and prestige were considered the lodestar to fame, power and fortune.

By 1903, however, in local Labour and trade union circles opposition had become crystallised in verbal and written protests because of his questionable company promotions. This Labour group was small in numbers and without funds for fighting an election, but while this hostility existed it was a threat to Bottomley's prospects and Horatio tried all the tricks he knew by letters and meetings, to win over these people. But they were neither to be cajoled or bought, and finally he tried the last trick. He brought a libel action against Mr Charles Horne, a working man, who was also secretary to the Hackney Trades Council. This libel action and its withdrawal is little referred to in the subsequent history of Bottomley's career. In fact, the case was in the pattern of Horatio's many legal efforts to silence his critics and, if adequately exploited, should have served to expose his future wiles. Mr Horne, it seems, had written a private letter to Mr Ben Tillett, the dockers' leader, ticking off the latter for consenting to speak at a public meeting of the Liberal Party in support of Bottomley's candidature. The libellous statement of Mr Horne's was that Tillett had allowed himself to be made the tool of an unscrupulous company promoter.

The part Tillett played in this affair does not redound to his credit. Tillet showed this letter to Bottomley. In his correspondence with the press in this connection, Tillett also referred to his Labour colleagues as "parasites", "hooligans", "gangs of incompetents" and "cadgers".

On 24 February, 1903, Bottomley demanded an apology from Horne under pain of either criminal or civil proceedings. No apology was forthcoming and a writ was issued, followed seven weeks later by a statement of claim. Immediately, the small band of working men set up a defence fund. Bottomley then tried to interview Horne to discuss "our political differences". Tillett wrote to Horne suggesting a meeting with Bottomley to thrash out matters concerning the libel action. As nothing came of this Bottomley said he would write to all prominent Labour leaders asking them not to support the defence fund but the letters were never sent. The statement of defence was delivered on 30 May, and the main pleas were pretty damning, if substantiated. The claim was that Bottomley had promoted 40 companies, nearly all of which had either gone into liquidation or been reconstituted. A one-man company, with a nominal share capital of £500, was used by Bottomley to promote four other companies with an aggregate capital of £3,375,000 and was used by him to manipulate the share market without regard for the interest of investors.

When Bottomley received this he took the extraordinary course of writing personally to Horne, rather than through his solicitors, calling upon him to withdraw and apologise. Horne never did so, and no answer was filed to the defence.

On 17 July an order of court was made directing Bottomley to set the action down for trial. He stalled, asking leave on three occasions to deliver a special reply to the defence, and then he asked for particulars of the companies to be supplied. The information was supplied on 1 September. Bottomley then made the remarkable discovery that the action, if proceeded with, would end in his having to pay heavy damages and decided to let the defendant off. This was all conveyed in a letter to the *Reynolds' Newspaper* for publication 14 days before Horne's solicitors were notified of Bottomley's intention to discontinue the case.

The defence fund raised £40 in small amounts from working men and associations who valued honesty in politics and Bottomley had to pay about £40 as taxed costs. Why was it that throughout his life Ben Tillett was a fellow traveller with Horatio and to be found on the same recruiting platforms waving the Union Jack in the 1914-18 War? He also pocketed a slice of the fees that they both received for their patriotic endeavours to get others to go out and fight — and die.

Twelve years after the Horne case a socialist named C.H. Norman published an article in the Glasgow *Forward* (later reprinted as a pamphlet) reciting details of Bottomley's gambling and financial schemes and shady practices. He commented that there was conclusive proof of the rottenness of British journalistic and political life when such a character as Horatio Bottomley was "consulted" by the rulers of the country. This was inviting prosecution from the litigious Bottomley who at first threatened to take proceedings but thought better of it and never did. He had a better plan up his sleeve. He had learnt his lesson in handling the Horne case and was not going into the box. He waited for the favourable opportunity to play his master stroke for which he had to find a stooge to help him. This came in 1918 when Horatio prosecuted a Birmingham printer John Greaney for republishing Norman's pamphlet. There was something odd about this case as no more than six copies were printed. Greaney was supported in court by a fellow Birmingham character, Reuben Bigland. Counsel for Greaney did not plead justification, arguing only for the amount of damages, which was agreed at £500. Thus the critics were silenced through the back door and future investigators into Bottomley's dubious financial affairs warned off.

But the sword of Damocles was waiting all the same in the hands of Rueben Bigland. In 1922, four years later, at Bottomley's Old Bailey trial, Bigland — in the role of crook turned penitent — related that he had paid Greaney £100 on behalf of Bottomley to republish Norman's pamphlet. Bottomley wanted no defence of the action and Greaney had agreed to put in a nominal defence so that Bottomley would only have to address the jury as to damages.

However, Bottomley's bankcruptcy in 1912 forced him to apply for the Chiltern Hundreds, and the political hold he had on South Hackney was broken. His trusty camp followers must have had a lean time until he started his Victory Bond racket but as Julian Symons writes in his excellent biography of Horatio Bottomley, the curious point about most of his camp followers was that few met comfortable deaths. I knew Perkins. In his heyday he was not stylishly dressed, but he was loquacious, leaning on the bar counter, standing drinks from the saloon bar of his favourite public house at the corner of Median Road, Clapton. Here he would be gathering and disseminating all the Bottomley news. Yet Perkins, after all the glitter and the limelight and his expense account of those many years on behalf of his master, was found dead by bailiffs in December 1935 in his back room at Median Road, not far from his favourite pub. He had been dead two weeks and had been living in extreme poverty.

Horatio after his release from prison was a broken man and a shadow of himself but firmly believing until his death that he was much misunderstood. I witnessed his rise and fall but he never swindled me of a penny — precisely because, knowing him when I was a boy, I never gave or lent him one. What he did do was to become president of our local Working Lads' Football Club, of which I was secretary when I was 15. Through his agent, our club (subscriptions 2d a week) received each year a present of a new football. This helped the working lads, whose wages in those days either as apprentices or errand and office boys ranged from 2s 6d to 8s a week, to play football matches on the rubbish dumps of Hackney Marshes.

Chapter 24

The outbreak of the 1914-18 War spelt the eventual disintegration of all the major socialist parties. This was a disaster after all the intense educational and propaganda work that had gone into the decade preceding the war. It was at the International Socialist Congress at Stuttgart in 1907 that, faced with the growing tension in European armament building, it was decided that the policy and duty of each national party should be one of attacking their own national governments for warlike and bellicose behaviour. The British SDF subscribed to this policy but it did not prevent some of its leaders, principally Hyndman and many other older socialists, developing Germanophobia. The war was also supported by Robert Blatchford. On all sides we could see the boiler pressures building up and no competent engineers at the safety valves. This division amongst the British socialist leadership meant eventually the death knell of the SDF and the passing of the *Clarion* and all its cultural and sports societies. Even the ILP, after the defection of Ramsay McDonald and Philip Snowden, became a shadow of its former greatness.

Another contributory factor was that the long continued period of unemployment after the war came to an end. But mostly, I think, the decline was caused by the formation of the Labour Party in 1918 on a constituency membership basis, aided by the trade union funds for electioneering purposes and the huge trade union block voting machine. This meant in the long run, as in other spheres of activity, the virtual trade union control of policy. The electoral machine, hitherto largely in the grip of the ILP, was gradually passing to the constituency Labour parties. The latter increased in membership and became geared solely to electioneering and the creation of a whole host of local councillors with a prestigious status to maintain. Thus the membership and influence of the purely socialist parties diminished and finally disappeared as an effective force.

As a young man at the time, taking an intelligent interest in public affairs, I experienced the astounding abysmal ignorance of the masses as to the real causes underlying the European situation. To talk to the ordinary citizens about foreign policy was like talking to them in a strange tongue beyond their immediate interest and comprehension.

When conscription of labour and men for the forces was imposed quite of number of young socialists like myself did not see eye to eye with our elders that it was "our duty" to be used as cannon fodder because a Parliament of old men had said so. The proletarian conscripts had no votes and no property to defend. What guarantees had they got beyond politicians' promises? "Homes fit for heros", "Equality of sacrifice", "Integrity of small nations", "Hang the Kaiser" and so on were just platform claptrap. And so thousands of doubting Thomases were hauled before military tribunals to prove they had a "conscience". The vast majority got short shift and were either bundled into prisons to cool off or hooked out of their jobs and "directed" to "work of national importance", usually to brickfields and other labouring work on a soldier's pay.

At my own appearance before the tribunal in 1916, I fared better than most since I was allowed to have my say. Whether it was my colossal cockney cheek or whether they thought that I would contaminate the ranks of the army with insidious proletarian propaganda I do not know.

I walked into the dock provided for the purpose in the Stratford Town Hall, and there before me on a raised dias were 14 bald-headed gentlemen, some rather rotund, but all looking as if they had done very well in their business. The chairman looked very regal seated in the elaborately carved and decorated mayoral chair.

The military man present, a major, got on to the mark at once. Didn't I think that this was a war to defend our country, its rights and liberties? "Half a minute, sir," said I. "Aren't you presuming a lot? What rights and liberties have I got? I never made the war and I've never been consulted about it. I haven't even got so much as a vote* and as much of this country as I own would go into a flower pot." He put to me a lot of hypothetical questions which got hypothetical answers which then got us nowhere. His further examination, mainly on patriotic lines, was like water on a duck's back but it enabled me to say a few things about my belief in a citizen army where all officers would be appointed from the ranks on merit without regard to their old school ties and my army would fight for the abolition of the class system in this country. I said the war had now entered upon a stage of attrition and its continuance by the aid of the working class would only lead to more widows and orphans, starvation and the workhouse. All this and more got the major out of his depth. He thought perhaps I had come to plead like so many religious "conchies" that it was wrong even to kill fleas and cockroaches. All I had in the world was my life and was that to be sacrificed fighting for the politicians' slogans, guaranteed five percent dividends on war loans, and

*At the time there were still some restrictions on male franchise. For example, the year-long residential qualification was not reduced to six months until 1918 and was not completely abolished until 1948. The author was not able to vote until he was 29.

eating in good hotels, while the Bill Browns and Joe Soaps on 1s 2d per day were wallowing in the mud of Flanders risking having their guts blown out and no real guarantees, if they were lucky enough to come back alive, to worthwhile jobs? This brought the chairman to remark: "I cannot understand this young man's mentality". It was quite understandable as there was about 50 years between us in age and a gulf in educational and social backgrounds. He was one of the Haves and I was one of the Have Nots and I was not going to the slaughter to preserve his privileges.

The prosperous businessmen, constituting my judges, decided I had a "conscience". They transferred my name to another government committee which decided, after another cross-examination, that my then employment, administering the Government's National Health and Unemployment Acts, was not "work of national importance". They also "directed" me to drop the pen and pick up a shovel, hoe or hod and work like a slave for a pittance.

This hard labour sentence was not going to be easy for me who tipped the scale at 8 st 6 lbs and was unused to hard physical labour. However, I packed an extra shirt, pants and vest, mounted my bicycle and prepared to journey forth into the broad acres of Merrie England.

The committee had sent me an early message to call on a potato farmer somewhere on the Dagenham Marshes, where council estates and the Ford Motor Works now stand. It was then a vast area of flat land with a huge barn in the centre of a sea of mud. The November morning was foggy and damp and I was none too cheerful at the prospect of working on such a dump. I was certainly up against reality. Pushing my bicycle carefully along the muddy cart track I reached the barn. This was stacked to the roof with hundreds of sacks of potatoes. I called out: "Anyone here?" A faint voice answered from the roof: "Wot d'yer want?". "I'm sent here for a job". "Orrite, load up them 'ere sacks of spuds on the waggon."

I tried to shift one sack of potatoes and it wouldn't budge. I turned round, got on my bicycle and rode away into the fog, leaving without a trace.

This early experience showed me that I should have to find my own labouring jobs and never attempt an ambitious project as to rival a dock labourer moving a two cwt sack of flour as if he was playing with a set of dominoes.

As a result of travelling around the farms I found that all the young intelligent and heftiest of the labourers had been flocking into Kitchener's army. Poor as the army pay and allowances were it was an escape from the miserable wages and conditions obtaining in labouring work and the hovels a great many had to live in. While the Forces were absorbing the fit and strong for cannon fodder the farmers, brickmakers and others had to depend on the old, the rejects and such labour as myself, ignorant of country ways and greenhorns when it came to manipulate the essential part of the milking cow.

I tackled the jobs as best I could but this meant I had always to be one jump ahead of that government committee sitting in Whitehall which was most anxious to push one of its labouring jobs on to me. Whenever I saw a village policeman taking tea with the farmer who had engaged me I surmised that enquiries were being made. Next morning found me taking off on my bicycle but usually leaving behind some wages.

Experience also taught me to engage myself as one who was travelling around gaining experience to become a farmer and who was willing to learn for pocket money. This suited many farmers, once I had shown them my employment card. Travelling took me into several counties and opened my eyes to the shortcomings of the so-called rationing system. Where I lodged in labourers' cottages rationing was paramount but where I could get my feet under the farmer's table there was no shortage of essential foods. They had arrangements with shopkeepers and the barter system came back under the counter.

Some farms were well managed, others were all mud, muck and mismanagement. One farm had the first of the milking machines in operation but the entrance to the stalls for the cows through the yard was an indescribable area of churned mud and manure. The cow's udders were wiped down it was true but how their milk got to London in a hygienic condition I never knew. This particular farmer spent most of his time travelling to and from race meetings, leaving his two sons to manage. They claimed exemption from the army as being "essential to the war effort". At 5 am each morning I would be out in the fields, which were waterlogged for the want of proper land drainage, calling and chasing the cows into the yard, where I had to stand at the gate and throw stones at the refractory ones before they would enter the cowshed, so thick and deep was the mud and slosh. Rubber wellington boots were unknown then and strong leather boots liberally cased in dubbin were no guarantee against continually wet feet. In fact, boots rotted away rather than wore away. Sitting down once to put the teat cups on a newly arrived cow, I suddenly received a hearty kick in the chest and found myself flying through the barn door and landing on my back in the yard of mud and manure. I carried the smell around for weeks. This farmer and I parted company because he thought I should only receive 18s per week instead of a pound he had first agreed to. Apparently his other two labourers wanted the same wages as myself and he was for downgrading and not upgrading. I was paying 15s per week for village lodgings and working 54 hours, Sundays included.

In Hertfordshire I worked on the biggest stack of hay I have ever seen, a 100 tonner so I was told. The weather was very hot. My task on top of that stack was to be under the elevator pitching the bundles of hay as they dropped to a man in the centre, who fed the man at the edges of the stack and all three of us were served by two men on the waggon below who were pitching the hay into the elevator's hopper whose merciless chain was driven by a rhythmic beat which came from the steam engine below. This was human automation, interfered with by occasional breaks to drink the beer we were allowed and then more sweat. Our beer allowance was seven pints a day on the stack and I reckon that I sweated that amount, too. We were never really drunk — only dizzy. Haymaking in our variable climate without the mechanical aids of today was a matter of skill, judgement and luck. It was always hard work.

I have seen stacks of hay when cut look as black as charcoal, a sure sign that the hay had overheated as a result of being stacked either too damp or too green. On one occasion I had to bore a hole with a large auger into the centre of a stack which showed signs of combustion. Through that hole came steam that had you sat over it would have cooked your rump as tender as a grilled steak in next to no time.

In Gloucestershire, instead of beer, the farmer handed out home made cider. I learned to brew this from his cider apples, placing them in a big stone circular trough and making a pony walk in circles, turning the mill stone. The juice went into a great vat, where it bubbled and squeaked. I never took to cider but old Sam Webb and Bill Simkins took a liking to working with me (incidentally regaling stories not fit for a drawing room) because they knew they were welcome to my daily allowance of cider.

The farm was called Mudham Farm and it lived up to its name for the mud was of a particularly sticky nature and when it rained it was everywhere. Sheep were kept on this farm and I had a sheep dog to help me from running my legs off in keeping the animals off the clover crop which "blows" them if they eat too much of it. When it came to dipping, treating them for foot rot or the maggot the task was not a pleasant one. Neither was it exactly hilarious when the winter mornings were bitterly cold and raw and I had to reset the fold on a freezing turnip field. Sometimes I would be out in the wide open spaces on a wet day so that the mud stuck like lumps of lead to my boots and I would cart and distribute mangel wurzels or bales of hay to store cattle. The wages were 16s a week, Sunday mornings included, plus a pokey little hovel agreeably called "a cottage", picturesque enough on the outside but inside smelling horribly of damp and mildew. When the winter commenced some of the labourers were put on piece work, hedge trimming, pulling mangels or dung spreading by the acre. Providing the weather was fair, they could manage to earn their 16s a week. Labourers on other farms I knew were not allowed to keep fowls, rabbits, a pig or even a dog so zealous were the farmers about pilferage from their stores, but wages paid did not encourage honesty.

There was some meanness and cruelty to animals. One farmer reproved me and threatened me with the sack for leaving around some saucers of milk for three half-starved cats that wandered about his barns. Their job, he said to me, was to catch mice and rats and find their own grub, but half-starved animals — and humans — were an abomination to me. He did not approve when I offered to pay for the small amount of milk they consumed so I carefully hid the saucers of milk after that, but he was rightly suspicious as those cats began to take an interest in following me around when milking time came along. I considered them as much a part of the establishment as his pigs for market but this fellow could see no further than his pocket.

There was one thing I never liked about farming and that was slaughtering the animals. I know it is necessary in a world of meat eaters and also pests have to be kept under control but the methods employed were primitive and revolting to me. Cattle droving on the roads to market involved long journeys and in the market pens there was a great deal of unnecessary cruelty. In the transport of horses for slaughter, too, I witnessed many sights that made me sick. Thank goodness we have more humane methods today.

During the last two years of the war, as I tended the sheep, fed the calves and pigs or hoed the turnips in the quietness of the countryside, I had an awful feeling of despondency. Would the carnage ever end? Had the civilised world gone stark, raving mad? I wondered, gazing at the skylark soaring into the blue with his song, was this the one lonely voice calling for reason and sanity? Over there in France men were slaughtering one another, but for what? That Czarist Russia should annex Constantinople, Great Britain should take parts of Persia and France should have Syria? This was treachery masquerading as diplomacy. It struck me then, as it did many other young proletarians, that we were in a world of chaos, a steaming cauldron of patriotism, heroism, imbecility, sadism, greed, self-righteousness, cant and humbug.

Chapter 25

The cessation of the war in November 1918 brought its disastrous aftermath for the working class: family upheavals, worsening of labour conditions and unemployment on an unprecedented scale. People were deluded into thinking that material conditions would be so much better after all the goodwill and human sacrifice that had gone into "our victory". It proved for the common people a hollow victory. As a result of sheer idiocy and incompetence, underlying the greed to "smash the enemy", no provision was made previously for the orderly reorganisation of industry or a planned economy to absorb the hundreds and thousands of service men clamouring to get back to their homes and families and start life afresh.

Before my experiences with the tribunal and my going on to the land, I had left my job in the legal world and got a job with the National Union of Sheet Metal Workers as a clerical worker.

Immediately after the Armistice I fled from the land and its miserable wages and journeyed back to London. Shortly after the war ended I married Grace, the daughter of an impecunious East End cabinet maker. Now we had nothing but two small suitcases and £10 between us and Queer Street. No employer was under any legal obligation to re-employ former employees who had been taken from them by conscription or who had volunteered. It was all left to work itself out in its own sweet way. All that demobilisation amounted to was soldiers walking round in circles in a jungle fighting for jobs.

I managed to get my job back. From then on for the next 25 years or so I administered the various insurance acts which were designed to cushion the effects of a bad social and economic system. My job was to listen to and advise the victims and the aged of their rights and benefits which they had helped to pay for.

My wife and I had rooms to find somewhere, anywhere in the vast metropolis living on a shoestring while waiting for the decision of my previous employers. We managed to find a couple of back rooms in a large house in Filey Avenue, Stamford Hill.

There were no facilities for cooking, except a gas ring. The tenants were a couple of young Jews under an agreement not to sub-let. It was impressed upon us that we should have to make ourselves scarce if visitors came. For our Sunday joint Grace did get permission to cook on their gas oven on Saturdays but the oven had to be completely scrubbed afterwards and the fact kept from their Orthodox Jewish parents as we were Gentiles. That gave us a little food for thought. Those parents arrived in this country penniless from the ghettoes of Poland to escape the pogroms; they had made money and were prosperous. Here we were two supplicants for two back rooms and a gas ring in our native borough, and here was the emergence of the race hatred trouble due to lack of housing.

Naturally, under the conditions we had to husband our resources when buying of furniture. The thought of hire purchase was against our principles; what we could not afford we could do without. This adaptability and co-operation made for a happy marriage but I think Grace carried it a bit too far after a month living like hermits. Arriving home one evening I found a huge Bryant and May's wooden case in the sideway. "What's this for?" I asked. "I've bought it for 6s at the oil shop; I want you to make me a larder cupboard with shelves", she said. So I had to get busy with a few tools and knock up a tolerable cupboard which served as firewood when we came to move.

It was love in two back rooms and the frying pan busy all the week; not idyllic perhaps but it taught us a few lessons to govern us thoroughly the rest of a long married life, one being not to worry too much about keeping up with the Joneses. Happiness, we found, was a state of mind and is not measured by surrounding oneselves with material comforts and gadgets, although these help. Neither can happiness be bought solely for cash. If you have the will to meet trouble squarely so well and good but if it appears insuperable — compromise.

Some time later we obtained a flat in a typical working class area in Adley Street, Marsh Hill, facing the Hackney Marshes. Occasionally, we had the smell from the soap factories at Stratford or the dust from "The shoot" as they filled in the Marsh with London's rubbish. Our next-door neighbour was one of Hackney's Labour mayors, William Parker. He was one-time leader of Hackney Council's Labour Group and a pioneer, like myself, in the Hackney Labour Representation Committee. He was what we called in the socialist and trade union movement of those early days one of the good old solids. He was a bitter opponent of Horatio Bottomley when the latter was courting South Hackney to become MP and who also helped to unmask that gentleman's shady company promotions many years before Horatio's Old Bailey trial and conviction.

William Parker and others, including myself, exposed a batch of smug, Bumble-minded shopkeepers and do-gooders, calling themselves the Hackney Board of Guardians because of their inhuman treatment of Poor Law recipients. There was one particular case we fastened on which was typical of those unfortunates who fell by the wayside because they contracted a serious illness and became unemployable. The man was named Tingey, a bricklayer who was unemployed. He fell ill and was forced to enter the Edmonton Infirmary. The Edmonton Guardians granted his wife and a family of nine children outdoor relief of 12s a week. As Tingey had lived in Hackney for 14 years, Edmonton Guardians claimed a refund of the 12s from Hackney, as they were entitled to do by law. The Hackney Guardians demanded that Tingey should be removed to their own infirmary in spite of the fact that he had a contagious disease and it was against the wishes of the Edmonton Infirmary doctor.

The Hackney Guardians insisted and refused to refund the grant unless Tingey came under their "care". Thus, they forced the whole family into the workhouse, where the cost was more than 16s a week for each inmate. The guardians deliberately broke up family life and the welfare of the whole family became chargeable to Hackney's ratepayers at a considerable cost.

Chapter 26

Members of the Sheet Metal Workers Union, for which I worked, belonged to a trade union which had existed under that name since 1823. In spite of the Combination Laws of 1799, which had been designed to prohibit and suppress trades unionism, it masqueraded under the title of the London Tin Plate Workers Pension and Funeral Society, and had a price agreement list for tinware with the employers in the trade dating back to 1797.

The craft of tin ware, with the development of industry, had, by 1918, developed into specialists manipulating all kinds of metals in branches of dairy implements, surgical instruments, gas meters, motor, Shipbuilding, ventilating, aircraft and so on.

I witnessed long queues of skilled men in the 1920s and 1930s eating their hearts out in a vain endeavour to find work; indeed, the task of placing them in the right place where there were ten good men for one available job was a headache, too. Yet I had to administer an imbecile government regulation which insisted that unemployed men should travel in circles to non-existent jobs, otherwise they ran the risk of losing their benefit on the ground that they were not looking for work. This was lunacy, concocted by statesmen at Whitehall. The only way a man could be proved an idler was to offer him a job. This the governments of the 20s and 30s would not face, hidebound as they were with age-old class prejudice. They could easily have initiated schemes of reclamation, house building and so much else as a social service with credit facilities rather than pay a dole to men and boys to hang about in idleness, sapping their morale and destructive of family life.

The administration at labour exchanges had a trying task so great and repetitive was their work. Occasionally one slipped into the sergeant major attitude towards the unfortunates who happened to be on the wrong side of the counter. I remember one fellow who threw his weight about at one exchange, overstepping the mark by barking at applicants. One day he slung a form back at an applicant whom I happened to know. "You haven't answered question 14", he barked. "Take the form and fill it up properly and take your turn at the end of the queue". The queue stretched well out into the street so the applicant quite mildly said: "But excuse me, what is question 14 about?". "Can't you read? Have you any dependants?" The applicant turned round to face the queue and in a loud voice so that all could hear said: "Chaps, this fellow here wants to know if I had any dependants. Of course I have — without us he wouldn't be here!"

In the 1920s besides having a mass of unemployed to deal with I also undertook on the NUC's behalf a survey of the country's trade union office staff. It was impossible to get adequate and satisfactory information — even from my own union, the Clerks — either as to rates of pay, methods of recruitment or whether every staff member — hold your horses! — held a trade union membership card.

The questionnaire provided me with some startling information, some of it not to the credit of the trade union movement. Some of the staffs were manned by non-unionists, all sorts of rates of pay and conditions operated, nepotism existed in some places, and there was no joint board machinery available for the settlement of a charter. Quite a number of the trade unions were doing approved society work under the National Insurance and Unemployment Acts and were extending their friendly society benefits side as a means of attracting and retaining members.

The survey showed the need for a clean-up on the unions' own doorstep, and so a few dedicated men and women got together and formed the National Trade Union Staffs Guild which eventually came within the framework of the National Union of Clerks. They appointed me as unpaid secretary and editor of the Guild's monthly journal, *The Eye Opener.* R.L. ''Bob'' Wigzell of the National Union of Railwaymen was president. We had a great measure of success in cleaning up the offices but not without a struggle with some general secretaries who thought that they should be the arbiters of what was good and what was not good for their clerks and administrators.

One union had an internal sit-down strike on its hands. When we met its executive committee, whose members had come from their workbenches to hear about the dispute, we reminded them that the organist might be rendering a masterpiece on the keyboard but they had to remember that down in the cellar was a relay of boys at the pump manually keeping the bellows going. They took the point.

In time the Staffs Guild fell foul of the parent union over the salary charter and broke away for a time and was refused recognition by the TUC which was understandable. The Staffs Guild embraced a policy of industrial unionism whereby all trade unions would merge into seven main industries, which would have guilds attached catering for their own special needs within the framework of their respective industry. This was too revolutionary for the times considering the vested interests, crafts, jealously as to who did what, cherished traditions to be broken up, and the general labouring unions and other unions organised on a geographical residential branch area basis.

Once the Staff Guilds executive committee had a meeting with Tom Mann, the pioneer of industrial unionism, when he became secretary of the Amalgamated Society of Engineers. It was about a salary claim by his Peckham head office staff. Our EC turned up, minus Sim Robertson, the ASE accountant and our principal witness for the staffs' case. Sim was the brother of the famous composer and founder of the Glasgow Orpheus Choir, Sir Hugh Robertson. A member of the staff side whispered to me that Sim had gone out on an important engagement that morning but had promised to be back for our conference. ''He'd better'', I said ''or we are sunk''. I passed a note to President Bob Wigzell: ''Do the charm stuff; stall on figures until Sim arrives''. Sim Robertson arrived as if nothing was amiss. I noticed he had a small brown paper parcel under his arm. He also had all the figures he wanted in his hand and never troubled to open the parcel wherein I imagined there was much memoranda beloved by all expert witnesses to impress, confound or inform the other side.

After the conference, the staff delegation adjourned to the nearest public bar for a drink. Sim, in his deer stalker hat and Harris Tweed jacket and trousers, excused himself as he said he wanted to get home early as he had married that morning. He sprung it on everybody just like that. ''Well'', I said, ''What's in the parcel, a bottle of whisky or some wedding cake to celebrate?''. ''Nae, laddie, just a sma' brown loaf and wee bit o' butter for our supper''.

If ever I had pretensions to soar to great heights of oratory, as I became more and more involved in meetings, I had early indications that as a speaker on the platform it was better I carried out the three great rules making a good chairman: stand up; speak up; and shut up. I thought my greatest strength and prestige lay with my flair in committee framing policy, organising propaganda, and administration. Being physically on the small side I was ever conscious that I might find myself laying down the law alongside fellows half as tall again and twice as fat and that would look ludicrous. I, therefore, left oratory and the showmanship that went with it to those best suited for the part.

I believe it was the late W. J. Brown of the Civil Service Union who once said that the ideal trade unionist must have the urbanity of a parson, the skill of a lawyer, the humour of a George Robey, the patience of an ox, the constitution of a bull, the capacity for being regarded as a scoundrel from the outset of his career to the end, and he must keep a smiling face through it all.

I have held all the unpaid offices of a trade union — chairman, secretary and any of the Uncle Tom Cobbleigh jobs that were going. For 25 years before 1943, I worked among paid officials and had personal dealings with dozens of shop stewards from the factory and the shopfloor. Whether I, being of common clay, possessed any of the qualities of men such as Mr Brown described never bothered me. What I do know is that during all those years the official breed never knew when or how they were able to get home to their beds before the milkman arrived. In truth, if they were too conscientious about their jobs they never knew domesticity for their lives were never their own. Now I believe that they all have cars, so perhaps things are different. We travelled across the city in trams, buses or by Shanks's pony often when there was a London pea souper, too.

Chapter 27

During the period of the war and for some time before, Grace and I had lived in the country. As I have said, after the First War we lived for a while at Stamford Hill and then moved to Hackney Marshes where we stayed for some years. But after, our experiences of country cycling convinced us that we should like to live somewhere quieter, less noisy, with less of the miles of brick and mortar fronting endless rows of uniform streets. In short, we began to hate living in London. If bread and butter compelled me to labour in town, at least we desired to sleep and enjoy our weekends in the air of the countryside. The problem opened up many possibilities and snags, all of which provided us with an endless topic of conversation, plans and ideas where, when and how.

We were familiar with the countryside, because I can say truthfully that one of the best periods of my life was the days I spent cycling through the Essex countryside before motor cars and lorries came to spoil it all.

The rural Essex I knew, with its gravel roads, in the days before the First World War, offered charm and adventure as well as punctured tyres. I preferred cycling in a group for the camaraderie it offered — a 20 mile run out and back on a Sunday gave me plenty to see and talk about.

The roads were dusty and gritty and the country pubs smelt of old timber and beer; there was the occasional puncture but there was always time to relax. At night we had to cope with paraffin or acetylene lamps.

In 1910 I had founded the North East London Clarion Cycling Club and when members were too numerous for safety on the road I founded various offshoots. Membership was open to both sexes and we explored the rustic villages and pubs for drinks and teas; there was plenty of bread and butter, cake, shrimps and lettuce. We rode two abreast with the captain in front and vice-captain at the rear, giving signals to one another by coded whistles. A puncture meant that two of us would drop out for the repair, the rest slowing down speed. Our journeys were accompanied by singing and the ringing of our bells — it was a real fraternal outing in the fresh air, far from the stinks and grime of East End life.

In those groups many found their marriage partners over the years. In the years after the clubs had ended, we celebrated with an annual dinner, remembering, too, those who had fallen in the war. These events carried on until the 1930s.

In our weekend cycling, visiting possible places and sites Grace and I came to the conclusion that the proposition of a country home would be a gamble in any case. We definitely ruled out entering into a mortgage even if that was possible in those days, as I feared I did not rank as having "sufficient security" in my job for a 20 year loan. In my young married days the sense of insecurity was very real however safe I felt at times; I was conscious of the hazards and risks being run with small hard-earned savings should sickness or unemployment strike me down.

We never gave up hope that we should somehow find an answer to the problem we had set ourselves. "I think", said Grace "that we should put first things first and buy some land on which to put up our own house". More easily said than done, I said, but it was the idea which finally dawned upon me that having savings locked up in land never seemed to waste but appreciated if anything as the pressures and community developed to give land its value.

Thus it came about we bought two and a half acres of land near Ongar in Essex in 1921, not that we had any intention at that time of building a house. We certainly thought a shed on it would realise a portion of our dreams to serve as a rendevous for cycle trips at weekends as we found that there were no rural planning laws against such temporary structures. Investing in a few carpentry tools I made myself a work bench which had a permanent place in the corner of the kitchen. During winter evenings I prepared in sections, ready for bolting together, a worthwile shed finally measuring 8ft by 16ft. With an eye to building our own bungalow as our ultimate object I practised all the points that I should most likely want when it came to the greater venture.

When all sections were ready and all other materials assembled in the garden, we hired an old Ford van one Easter Friday and transported the lot to the site, not without a couple of engine breakdowns on the road to give us a few qualms as to whether we should arrive with everything intact. We had been going down to the site at weekends and constructed the concrete footings, thus taking our first practical steps in marking out, mixing concrete with the right aggregates. Grace carried the water and poured it, between making meals and tea, while I did the shovelling, turning the stuff and pouring cement into the trenches. We also built a brick fireplace, our first lesson as to how bricks should be properly laid and plumbed. That Easter "holiday" of four days physically hard work, assembling, fixing, erecting, tailing and bolting the shed together left us tired and weary to cycle the 20 miles home. We felt, however, a sense of achievement and contentment that we had surmounted the first hurdle in our life's ambition. Our joy, though, was short lived. A telegram arrived, sent by a villager: "Gale dislodged shed from footings". This was the same gale that brought the Airship, R 101, to disaster with the loss of many lives.

I was conscious that I had taken a calulated risk inasmuch as I had had no time to pin the wall plates to the concrete footings. On arrival at the site the following weekend the damage was not as great as we might have expected. The gale had shifted the building as a whole a few inches off the corner of the footings and smashed a couple of large sheets of asbestos coverings. By leverage, we soon got the shed back where it belonged. Considering the violence of the gale my carpentry joints had stood up well to the test. Had we relied upon nails and flush joints the whole thing would have collapsed like a pack of cards.

We divided the shed into two parts, one for sleeping and the other for cooking and taking our ease. For a few years we enjoyed our weekends in the country. This added to our determination to prepare ourselves to take the plunge and go for a permanent dwelling against the time some form of transport came to the village to take me backwards and forwards to London. On our cycle journeys at weekends we called on building sites inspecting the various stages of construction to accustom ourselves as to what we should be up against when it came to building the real dream bungalow. We even prepared various models to scale in match sticks and cardboard in order to work out specifications, quantities and lay out of rooms and furniture. Later on we left this technical side to an architect friend.

We knew from the start that it would be a gamble and disastrous should I fall sick or unemployed at a stage when the walls were half way up but faith can move mountains we are told. Our estimate of the cost without labour was around £358 and we had nowhere near that sum. We just hoped to get through the final stages of building our bungalow by working in slow motion on my monthly salary. So it came about a few days before the General Strike was declared in May 1926 that we sent off our first order to the local gravel pits to deliver 30 yards of ballast and 20 yards of sand at 8s a cubic yard. The die had been cast and there could be no going back. It now meant work, hard work, for every weekend and holiday period over the following two and a half years before the bungalow was fit to live in and qualify for the government subsidy of £75.

A well had to be sunk for domestic purposes. This we left to a local man who had been a miner and who assured us that anywhere in Essex a tolerable supply of water could be found at around 20 feet. To make sure of the spot he walked around with a hazel twig and when his wrist pulled he marked the spot with a stick. As luck would have it the spot was near where we wanted the bungalow built so we had the well piped to supply a tank in the roof of the bungalow and installed a pump for that purpose over the kitchen sink. Our ex-miner wanted £10 plus 10s a foot below the 20 feet depth and we were to supply the bricks. He and his boy cut down through the London clay at an alarming speed in three days. He did this without shoring which I thought was some risk as I had heard of wells caving in. The usual method we were told was to use a large cartwheel as a template and proceed to lay bricks without cement as each foot of clay was cut away from underneath the wheel allowing the whole to gradually sink. At 22 feet a smaller hole was dug in the centre of the clay and by next morning it was seen to be full of water and the digger then knew he had struck the water stratum; the water pressure from the outside caused water to percolate into the well. During the whole of the 30 years that well was in use only on two occasions — and then in drought — did we have to ration ourself. For all other occasions such as baths, watering stock and garden, we had taken the precaution of having a number of 100 gallon tanks to catch all rain water from the roofs of the bungalow and outbuildings.

One Christmas there was a heavy fall of snow and the day after Boxing Day there was very little traffic on the roads. Grace and I were compelled to walk the five miles into Brentwood already tired and weary from our work on the chimney stack. We slumped into the coach at Brentwood and slept all the way to Bow Bridge when we had to be awakened by the conductor.

By now all our savings had been spent and we still had an estimated year to continue working on a limited budget of what we could spare from a monthly salary. Truly it was a period of tightening the belt, but also there was a firm determination that there could be no retreat. We finally achieved our goal by September 1928. We christened our home "Smallburgh", after my grandmother's native Norfolk village.

We lived in the house until 1955 and never tired of the 10 mile view from our windows across the Roding Valley to Epping Forest, a view of undulating country and only two farmhouses to signify that we did have distant neighbours. The sky above was the flight path of thousands of rooks, wheeling, turning and cascading in the air as they winged their way each evening to their roosting rendezvous in Epping Forest.

As our land sloped sharply away to the south west from the bungalow, Grace decided it was a time-wasting job and also a strain on her vocal chords to hail me should I be at the bottom of the slope. She solved her problem by buying a hunting horn on which she would blow three blasts from the window when she required my attendance. This trumpet call set a fashion on all the other smallholdings, each one having its own "call sign" from a ship's bell to banging on a common dustbin lid.

We always had on our table all kinds of fruit. Some of the fruit trees I grafted myself. We made jams, preserves and grew vegetables all the year round, even attempting a little wine making. We had eggs, poultry, rabbits and geese. We even bred goldfish in our lily pond. This pond we set in a sunken garden, measuring 60 feet by 40 feet, flanked by four majestic cypress trees and a weeping willow, all grown from slips taken in the early years of our occupation.

In 1940 or thereabouts, in response to the Government appeal to plant pockets of waste land with timber trees because of the devastation of country woodlands, we planted a coppice of about 650 saplings which I had sent down from Elgin in Scotland. They were still growing stoutly in 1955 when we left.

Until 1954 we were without piped water, gas, electricity or the telephone. We managed with cesspool drainage and bottled gas. By the following year we had the benefit of all services and "Smallburgh" was an established homestead but needed labour to keep it going. At our age the time was ripe for selling. It had cost us £350 for materials and comparable bungalows at the time that it was built were selling for £750. We sold it for £2,100.

Chapter 28

In 1930 I was still working as chief clerk to the sheet metal workers' union and I continued in this job until the Second World War. In 1940 call-up was introduced and, being 50 years of age, I was exempted, while offices were being combed for recruits.

On the union staff was a young fellow whose services the general secretary wished to retain. The latter conceived of a plan whereby I would relinquish my job and status (but without loss of pay) and then the other fellow would be promoted in my stead placing him in an exempted position.

When I refused to countenance this I fell out of favour with the general secretary. The plan played on my mind so much, in fact, that I suffered a nervous breakdown and walked out of the job. My enforced six month rest with my nervous trouble saved my sanity. Eventually I was to find work with the Essex County Council but before I move on I must relate how I, who had spent a quarter of a century advising others about their benefits and rights, fell foul of the evils of the then still-existent Poor Law.

Despite the reforms, which had begun with the introduction of National Insurance in 1911 by Lloyd George, the concepts behind the Poor Law were the same as ever: there was a strong element of deterrence, means testing and what was called "chargeability". And even in 1940, with the country supposedly pulling together against Hitler, the Poor Law attitudes were being shown toward the victims of the bombing raids on London. Until Hitler's air force started in earnest in that year to bomb the capital, the Government had based all its relief measures for civilian casualties, homeless persons and others on the Poor Law pattern of administration. To all intents and purposes they handed the job to Poor Law officials, who in their turn recruited voluntary aid from bodies like the Women's Voluntary Service, which helped with rest centres and catering and similar work.

The voluntary workers brought a breath of fresh air into the organisation as they had little or no attachment to the niceties of Bumbledom and the mass of legalistic rubbish and precedents accumulated from the time of the first Queen Elizabeth when the Poor Law came into being. Little did I think that I would challenge authority and the whole edifice of guardian procedure in a personal capacity. All my life I had been challenging it for other people; now it was thrust upon me to do it for myself.

When, on the 30 August, 1940, Goering sent his bombers on their opening raids on the dock area of East London, my mother, sister and brother-in-law were amongst the first to suffer. My mother was so badly shaken up when taken out of the garden shelter that she had to be taken away in an ambulance. She was then 86. For 48 hours such was the devastation and confusion that no one could tell me exactly where she had been removed to. The poor woman next door had been killed and when I saw the garden shelter it had been twisted like a corkscrew. Streets of houses round about had been flattened. Eventually matters were clearer and I was told that mother was alive and in the Leytonstone Infirmary. Within a month that infirmary was bombed twice. On the last occasion, Block S was completely demolished and mother only saved by a heavy door falling across her bed and thus protecting her from falling bricks and rubble. All she would say when I saw her after this ordeal, with characteristic coolness, was; "That bugger Hitler has been here again". Later, my sister Alice and her husband, Joe Hayward, were bombed out three times from their temporary homes and yet they still stuck to their beloved Plaistow to the end.

But in all this courage and fortitude there were sustained efforts by the Poor Law officials, acting under orders from above, to pin on me that as an only son I was responsible under the Poor Law Act for the cost of maintenance of my mother while in their institution. They said she was homeless and, therefore, destitute. I said her trouble was her age and that after the bombing ordeal she was in need of nursing and care. This the family could no longer give her. My sister had been bombed out and was in a temporary shelter. As for myself I was doing war work and my wife was in Ongar Hospital after a major internal operation. The welfare authorities of West Ham sent me a form asking for the fullest details of my income and employers. They wanted to know if I had lodgers and what did they pay, as well as my wife's income. The leading question, the kick in the donkey's hind hoof, was left until the last and printed in heavy type: "What weekly sum are you prepared to pay?" I wrote: "Nothing". They replied by sending me in a bill for £16 2s being eight weeks at £2 0s 3d a week. I ignored the bill and their letter. At that time I had enough on my plate — both wife and mother in hospital; I was travelling 52 miles a day to and from business, dodging air raid bombing; and doing a stint of fire watching.

Then came another letter — would I attend the guardians for an interview? I did so, and unburdened myself to them. I said I was not trying to evade my responsibilities towards my mother as both my two sisters and myself had been providing for her before the bombing happened. It was a matter of principle with me that mother was where she was as a result of Hitler's action and until such time as we could bring him to account it was the nation's job to look after the fallen and it should not be upon the individual family. They recognised all this "but it is the law''. So I said that the law could go and hang and I was prepared to face a public prosecution and would see that I got the maximum amount of publicity to shift the Government to change the law as it was unfair and an injustice towards those who were in the front line. If the Government persisted in applying the ''chargeability'' Poor Law rule plus the means test, I said that we should find ourselves as the bombing developed faced with hosts of people evacuating to safer areas as a great many were doing, and no one could blame them, but those who stayed behind facing the hell fire and their war work would be doubly penalised for their family casualties. Was this not playing into Hitler's hands? The guardians told me that I was first to raise this issue and while they were sympathetic, I had nevertheless placed them in an embarrassing situation because of a result of the continued devastating bombing in their area, hundreds of other homeless people were becoming ''chargeable''.

It was at this time I happened to be the unpaid secretary to the Chelmsford Divisional Labour Party. I wrote to Clem Attlee, the Labour Deputy Prime Minister, putting my case and offering my opinion that the Government would be well advised to review the Poor Law regulations concerning the growing number of civilian war casualties. His reply was short and sharp: the terms of the coalition between the parties was that there would be a standstill on legislation; therefore, he could not see how things could be altered however much he regretted my domestic troubles.

I never paid the bill and the guardians pressed no more. At least I thought so for they were waiting nevertheless. Mother, like the traditional old soldier, gradually faded away. When the welfare department were notified of her death the town clerk sent a letter to me reminding me of all the rigmarole regarding ''chargeability'' and calmly informing me that they had a legal claim against any money or estate left by Elizabeth Southgate, deceased. He requested, by return, to know the cost of her funeral, who paid and the name of the undertaker, the amount of insurance, who received it, the name of the insurance company and whether my mother had left any other money or property.

So the ghouls had been biding their time, waiting at the graveyard to pounce on an old lady's few possessions. Was this a grim joke, a macabre sort of humour since all my dear old mother had was blown skyhigh in that air raid of 30 August 1940? None of the family were mercenary enough to put in a claim for them. I was at first inclined to ignore this but instead I told the clerk I thought we were fighting a war as a nation and not as individuals who were expected to pay for their own casualties out of their own pockets. I also told him that, apart from my mother's old age pension (which the authority had received while she was in their care), my two sisters and I had supported her. I had no insurance on her life and I had paid all the funeral expenses and my mother had died as poor as she had been born 88 years before.

This did not satisfy the Poor Law mind in the midst of a raging war. When my sister asked for the return of her mother's wedding ring, purely for sentimental reasons, she was told that the guardians would be holding this under ''chargeability''. I called on the official (I think that they had had enough of me) and he agreed to release it to my sister. The ring was a thin gold band that mother had worn (and pawned) for 70 long years.

Chapter 29

I resigned my job with the Sheet Metal Workers Union in 1943. I was able later to get a job with Essex County Council in a war-time capacity as an assistant rest centre officer. The work entailed looking after bombed-out homeless people, inspecting and keeping up to standard all the paraphenalia, food and medical stores connected with a number of rest centres in an area which stretched from Brentwood to Burnham-on-Crouch. Each local centre was run by members of the Women's Voluntary Service under the control of a local officer of the Poor Law department.

Hughie Griggs was the group officer and I was his assistant. He did his job well and conscientiously. I was glad to work with such a colleague in all our ''incidents'' — the description of the bombings. We also had to organise mock incidents to train our voluntary workers what to do, when and if they had to tackle the real thing. Neither Hughie nor I had the traditional Poor Law-type of mind in handling the homeless and consequently we had the minimum of trouble in dealing with difficult situations where sometimes diplomacy and tact were needed to handle people dispossessed of their homes and in a state of panic and distress. I'm afraid that in giving this help at times we forgot a lot of red tape of which the powers that be were constantly reminding us. We were told, for example, how many cups of tea should be served from a ½lb packet of tea.

Hughie was tall and heavily built whereas I was short and slim, ''the long and short of it'', some wag dubbed us as we walked into a centre together, a quip we all enjoyed and thus put everyone at their ease. Hughie was a lady charmer and musical, and I was, dare I say it, efficient and full of cockney repartee — assets in our work to keep the homeless from brooding too long over their immediate troubles.

The disastrous effect of putting a Poor Law officer of the old school in charge of a rest centre was experienced once, when Hughie and I were deputed to take over a centre in East London at short notice. Every hour or so Doodle Bugs were screaming over the area towards their targets; occasionally, one would shut off its engine and then there would be the tense moment wondering and waiting for the explosive crash.

When we entered this particular centre, we were amazed to find a long queue of people filing round the walls of a one-time casual ward. The place was not inviting, the lighting poor, the walls whitewashed, the odour of sleeping bodies coming from a set of cubicles partitioned off with blankets at the far end of the place. Meals of a sort were being served in the same hall.

The people were waiting their turn to reach an elderly fellow sitting on a high chair at a high desk. He was handing out tickets to each person, entering their names on a sheet of paper. The ticket holder would then go to a table where there were some ladies handing out a meal in return for the ticket.

"What the deuce is going on here?" enquired Hughie looking down at me. "That's the old Poor Law procedure for tramps in casual wards", I replied. The tickets were a check on the number of meals supplied for there were no second helpings in a casual ward.

Hughie was furious and off he went to find the lady who he was told was the leader of the voluntary workers. Meanwhile I had my job to do and milled around asking questions of the homeless trying to get the feelings of the occupants who seemed to agree that the place was a dump and the food not much better. There was a mixture of despair and sullen anger amongst the 80 unfortunates who had been directed there to await rehousing.

The old gentleman on the high desk was, as I guessed, the local relieving officer, brought up in the old school, looking upon all homeless as tramps, workshys or rogues, who had to be watched and docketed.

Hughie had been sent down to take over from him. The vicar's wife was almost in tears when found, complaining bitterly that she had in no way been helped by "that sick old man up there". I described my feelings — the lamentable state of the larder and food stores incapable of feeding the number we had to cater for and suggesting that a jolly good meal was necessary to quiet matters down. To supplant an old Poor Law servant required diplomacy and this was achieved by calling in a local doctor to advise the old man to take a rest.

In the meantime, I made out the requisition orders on local tradesmen. The food arrived, the ladies got busy and by nine o'clock that night we gave everyone an honest to goodness meal with no tickets, no queueing, no fuss and served second helpings. For breakfast next morning we had eggs and bacon contrary to regulations but we had established a little more tranquillity, if such was possible in a rest centre with Doodle Bugs dropping about one's ears every hour or so.

Hughie and myself, with a girl clerk, were the only full-time rest centre staff looking after an area covering a large slice of south eastern Essex, known as Group 9 on the Essex Poor Law map. Everything was run on a shoestring, understandably so, with all the other government commitments to fight Hitler to the last ditch with blood, sweat and tears. The whole organisation of relief and care of the homeless, based as it was on the archaic Poor Law pattern with some of the old time Poor Law officials with Victorian attitudes of mind towards poverty in charge, would have collapsed had Goering's bombers got the upper hand of our own valiant RAF in the defence of London. As it turned out we had to rely on voluntary help but these helpers never let us down.

And what of those bombed-out citizens? They, too, responded with fortitude and courage when some of their homes lay in ruins and in cases had lost dear ones amongst the rubble. War, it has been said, can bring out the worst as well as the best in us. It was hectic at times also coping with shortages of nearly everything, especially essential foods, but in all that and all the suffering the best was often to be seen.

Chapter 30

After the war had ended and this work came to an end the county council continued to employ me in helping to wind up and dispose of the huge war-time surplus stores that had accumulated in the various depots. When this was done they found they had no further use for me. I was given a nice letter of thanks and good wishes for my future. I was 55 at the time and as far as helping me get another job the letter wasn't worth the paper it was written on. The rule that applicants of 50 were too old for a job was being applied.

And so followed 18 months of unemployment with no illusions as to what to expect from war-time promises about a new world. I had no illusions about the labour exchange. I looked to them only to pay me my £2 a week benefit, the first time that I had claimed in all the years that I had paid my contributions.

I remember that the exchange sent me to a ganger's job in charge of a team of platelayers on the old LNER railway in the depths of winter, and on another occasion it was a labourer's job that I was offered, loading and shovelling broken glass into a furnace hot enough when I went near it to frizzle your shirt in a minute. Another way to find a job, with which I became conversant, was that of filling in an application form at the work's gates and then waiting for an interview, with little chance of getting one, but I never fell for that. I was also sent to a private airfield to try for a timekeeper's job but again my age let me down.

Experiences like this could make one cynical of interviews and always the same end product — a letter saying: "Sorry". To many men of my age in similar circumstances this could have bred despair and frustration. But at least I owned the roof over my head and could go into my own garden and find a meal, but what of the thousands not so fortunate?

By the time my second Christmas of unemployment came around, I was near the end of my entitlement to benefit and I would be classified among the unemployable. Even temporary work at Christmas in the Post Office sorting office was denied me, though it was not denied to grammar school boys and girls at a shilling an hour.

I began now to realise that I had reached the cross roads when a decision would have to be made. What was it to be? Would I be in idleness, seeing the slow attrition of our life's savings, public assistance, the means test and the rest of the cap-in-hand indignities, or should I explore the uncharted path of becoming a self-employed man and, with a bit of luck and grit, win through?

Neighbours gave me many little handyman jobs to do. This gave me a clue to the right path to follow and stopped me tilting at too many windmills. Yes, I would go back to the land but on my own terms. I would couple this with any casual handyman work offered and within the compass of my abilities. This was a new sort of freedom. I could pick and choose work suitable to my physical capacity and take a day off when the flesh and the devil beckoned me. Neither Grace nor myself were great lovers of chasing the almighty dollar and we were immune from the social worries of trying to keep up with the Joneses so that it did not prove a difficult task. The skills and knowledge of country life which I had learned would serve without the difficulties caused by long hours in inclement weather. When it became generally known that my services were available as a handyman, builder, gardener and the like and that I had a record that I never scamped a job, I can honestly say I never looked back. If there had been eight days in every week and sleep was unnecessary, I could at times have filled every minute. But I never lost sight of my cardinal rule — money isn't everything.

As a jobbing gardener, my day-to-day employers would be mainly middle class people with money to spend on the upkeep of their gardens. Among them I found occasionally the "oddities" as I called them, particularly the elderly spinsters. One of these was a dedicated churchgoer with a flair for helping foreign Bible missions, her pet one being proselytizing amongst the Eskimoes of the Far North. She would call an annual gathering at her spacious home and garden of all her friends to collect funds for this purpose. Her domestic staff were included and were given half a crown each to put into the collecting bag as it came round so that no one escaped this well-intended effort to save the Eskimoes near the freezing North Pole from the eternal fires of hell.

When Christmas came round she stopped her usual Christmas box of 10s to each of her domestic staff on the ground that a rapacious government was robbing her by taxation. She went on providing spiritual guidance to the Eskimoes but could still depart for a six week holiday leaving her 80 year-old cook to come in daily to feed her three cats, without paying her part wages.

During the 16 years that I was engaged in gardening and working as a handyman I was happy and interested. The multiplicity of tasks and the variety of work gave me infinite pleasure, largely because it appealed to my creative nature. At times I would be asked to make a lawn or a tennis court where once a mess of uneven mounds of weeds and rubbish existed; a green house might be needed to be built, repaired or reglazed; a specimen tree of Hisakura cherry or a Prunus Pissardii Nigra planted out on a lawn with a small rock garden in the background. There were the larger tasks — planting two acres of Cox's apples in line formation trees, intercropped with blackcurrant bushes. I pruned 7,000 fruit trees, built chimney stacks, felled trees, reared calves and pigs, milked cows, and bred poultry, geese and rabbits. I took out a motor scythe to reclaim derelict orchards and, generally, made hay while the sun shone. All this was more pleasurable than balancing books or paying out dole money, even if the money I could make from such work was not great.

But the tragedy of my story is in the tail. On the day after I had signed the contract to sell "Smallburgh", Grace met with a cycling accident and broke her left thigh bone. From this she never recovered, went into decline and died four years later at the age of 73.

Without her loving help and goodness I could never have accomplished a tithe of what was done. Throughout our lives we had tried to be creative in spirit as well as in deed, hating injustice and humbug, bearing malice against no one. It has been an eventful life, I think, but I leave you, reader, to be my judge.

Last words
Terry Philpot

It is more than 20 years since Walter Southgate completed the writing of this book. He wrote it when even then he was able to look back on a long life, and drew it to a close with the death of his wife. She had been his companion in arms for more than 40 years, and they had sold the smallholding which they had worked together since 1921 and which had been their home for almost as long.

Grace Southgate died in 1959 having lived, in poor health, for four years in their new home at Harold Park, a small, cosy bungalow, with a sweeping expanse of garden. While he continued to care for her at the end of her life, Walter Southgate also, despite his advancing years, continued to work. As he relates, as a jobbing gardener he was able to put to use the skills and experience which the young East Londoner had first acquired as a fugitive conscientious objector in the First World War and which he had perfected when he and his wife had decided soon after that to take to the land at Kelvedon Hatch.

Laying out orchards, landscaping, doing handiwork, pruning and planting fruit trees and cultivating gardens for fruit, vegetables and flowers must have seemed a long way from his urban, concrete boyhood and youth. But it satisfied what he had wanted from life; as he had shared the vision of a better world offered by the early socialist movement, as he had raised up his small voice against the universal horrors of the Great War, as he had worked for and sought fellowship in bodies like the Clarion Movement, so did his new trade satisfy a wish to be at best creative and at very least not destructive. It was a modest but personal contribution to wider forces.

Taking up professional gardening did not mean, however, that he forsook his early beliefs or ceased his activities. In these last two decades he was for five years secretary of the Harold Wood Labour Party; and he helped to found and was for 12 years vice-president of the Havering Humanist Society, carrying on a secularist tradition imbibed from his father whose portrait he paints so vividly in the book. He was also vice-president of the Romford Historical Society. When, finally in 1965, at the age of 75, he decided that the time had come to retire, he was able to give more time to these activities. He wrote the occasional article and gave talks and continues to do so at the age of 91, travelling to places as far from home as Brighton and Ruskin College, Oxford. In 1978 he was presented by Prime Minister James Callaghan at the Labour Party conference the National Executive Committee's Certificate of Merit for "outstanding voluntary service to the Labour Party".

There was one job he never retired from — quill pen making. That was a skill which he had taken in with paternal politics and secularism. His father was the last professional quill pen maker, and although he had not wanted his son to follow him in what he could see was a dying trade, Walter Southgate picked up the art from watching his father.

As it is, the work is still called for. Lloyds of London have a 250 year old tradition of making entries in their wrecks book with such pens. When the Lutine Bell rings to announce the loss of a ship, work does not begin again until the entry is made. The firm sought out Walter Southgate and he has supplied them with pens since his father's death in 1919. He works with a century-old penknife, inherited from his father. Using the wing feathers of a moulted wild goose or a swan or a mature turkey for the best quality pens, the feathers have first to be treated or baked in silver sand to harden (''dutch'') them and make them opaque and hard enough for cutting into a finely shaped nib. He also uses the pens for his hobby — he took up calligraphy at the age of 65 and has produced some colourful and beautifully executed pieces.

However, it is also in the last 20 years that has come into being the result of more than 70 years quiet but persistent agitation. When in 1975 the National Museum of Labour History was opened by the then Prime Minister Harold Wilson, Walter Southgate was present not only as one of the founding members — no mean achievement as that was — but also as the donor of the largest single collection in the museum, a massive and most extraordinary and priceless number of items. And yet on that subject, of how a boyish pastime grew into almost an obsession which helped to give the country one of its newest and most unusual museums, the autobiography is strangely silent. The story needs telling here.

Walter Southgate's paternal grandmother had begun a scrapbook in the 1840s. In it she pasted cuttings, photographs, cards and illustrations, recording in haphazard and personal fashion, the events of her own lifetime. Her grandson never knew her but his father, who, as we have learned, was someone who didn't place much value on such things, preferring to consign them to dark cupboards and forget about them, gave the book to his son. Although, as the autobiography tells us, the family was in no way religious, it did observe Sunday in what we may now think a rather cheerless manner: the children were not allowed to play or sing, to read or indeed to do much to make their presence felt at all. Quietness and a rather grey solemnity was the order of the Sabbatarian Sunday, except that the young Southgate was allowed to look through the colourful pages of his grandmother's scrapbook.

His grandmother's taste for the unusual, for the item that in some way illustrated the contemporary event or person was inherited by her grandson, and at about the time when he tells us he became involved with the Social Democratic Federation in 1905 he also began collecting whatever took his fancy — handbills, posters, pamphlets, books, personalia. At lunchtimes the boy in the lawyer's office took himself off to the bookstalls that were to be found in the market which then strung itself along Shoreditch High Street. A first edition of Thomas Paine's *Rights of Man,* with notes on his trial for treason, bought for just sixpence, was but one early item that 70 years later found its way into the museum. Many of the items were acquired not by advertising for them and paying big prices but by Walter Southgate being known as a collector, keeping an ever-watchful eye, and a little luck. The inscribed watch which once belonged to Tom Jones, first organising secretary of the London Trades Council in 1861, and which has, sadly, been stolen from the museum, was purchased from a friend for £6.

As he began collecting the idea of a small museum devoted to the history of the Labour movement occured to him. The first person he approached was the historian G D H Cole, whose widow, another historian the late Dame Margaret Cole, was coincidentally to become a trustee of the museum. He liked the idea but was, he said, too busy to pursue it further. The story was one to recur time and time again — trades councils, local Labour parties, the trade unions, none had the time to help. But all the while much was being lost through neglect, export and thoughtless sale. (In recent years the table upon which Paine wrote *The Rights of Man* and a volume of Woolmer's *Black Dwarf* have only just been saved from being exported; the museum has the table and a copy of the newspaper can also be seen there.)

And yet Sidney and Beatrice Webb, writing in their *History of Trade Unionism* as long ago as 1890, had said: "In many a working man's home in London and Liverpool, Newcastle and Dublin — above all Glasgow and Manchester — the descendants of the old skilled craftsmen have unearthed 'grandfather's indentures', or 'father's old card', or a tattered set of rules to help forward the investigation of a stranger whom they dimly recognise as striving to record the annals of their class."

Alas, there were too few who gave recognition to the irreplaceable value of such things. As Stan Newens explains in his foreword, it is only in comparatively recent years that there has come about a more general and wider understanding of the importance of the lives of ordinary men and women in analysing those larger historical trends and movements. In this the historical bric-à-brac and personalia are powerfully and fascinatingly illuminating. We are fortunate that Walter Southgate had the interest and prescience to go against the grain of too many of his contemporaries.

But it was not until 1963 that he came upon others who were as passionately interested as he in providing a permanent home for all this and much more. He came in contact at that time with a like-minded group of people in Reigate in Surrey. Among them were Henry Fry, Charles Pearce, Richard West and Florence Willard. In 1966 a small exhibition of Labour history was mounted in the town by the Reigate Town Council and the Socialist History Society. In that year, too, the enthusiasts came together to found the Trade Union, Labour, Co-operative, Democratic History Society (TULC) and it was then that Walter Southgate made over to that body (along with £800 to further its aims) his collection which by then amounted to 600 items, including posters, photographs, books and furniture.

Walter Southgate became the organisation's membership secretary, holding the post until 1978. The agitation continued. TULC's numbers were never large, its organisation never widespread nor sophisticated, but it became known, its credentials were established, it had the interest of the TUC and trade unions like the Transport & General Workers Union. By the time that the museum was opened, with the assistance of Tower Hamlets Council, other large collections, including those of the Socialist Sunday School movement and the National Council of Labour Colleges had been added.

The museum is situated in a borough whose wider boundaries take in the area where Walter Southgate was born. The old slums have long gone, although some of the environment is recognisable to the very elderly. He has painted a lively picture of the terrible material poverty lightened by the richness of the community and its life — the local characters, the sense of family, the woman who would pawn her wedding ring time and time again to help a neighbour suffering hardship.

Much of what he describes may seem worlds apart — from that community to the once worldwide Clarion movement; from the travails of a conscientious objector on the run in the First World War to the life that could be had by the industrious smallholder who for some effort and not too much money was willing to chance his lot in an unspoiled countryside and unrestricted by modern planning regulations; and from a boy sorting through the stalls of East End markets to the street corner agitation of little socialist groups. And all that is itself worlds away from the society which has replaced it. What binds it together is to be found in one life recorded between these covers.